Legal Research
in
North Carolina

Legal Research
in
North Carolina

Miriam J. Baer

Edited by
James C. Ray

CAROLINA ACADEMIC PRESS
Durham, North Carolina

Library of Congress Cataloging-in-Publication Data

Baer, Miriam.
A guide to legal research in North Carolina / by Miriam Baer.
    p. cm.
Includes bibliographical references and index.
ISBN 1-59460-008-2 (alk. paper)
1. Legal research--North Carolina. I. Title.

KFN7475.B34 2005
340'.072'0756--dc22   2005015359

CAROLINA ACADEMIC PRESS
700 Kent Street
Durham, North Carolina 27701
Telephone (919) 489-7486
Fax (919) 493-5668
www.cap-press.com

Printed in the United States of America

Contents

Introduction

Who is in charge if the President and Vice President of the United States are killed in a terrorist attack? Does North Carolina recognize gay marriage? Is it a crime to write a bad check? You may not know the answers to all of these questions, but you can find them if you know how to do legal research.

Whether you prefer turning a page or typing on a keyboard, there is a host of information available to you about the law, once you learn the skills to find it. This book will give you the basics. Read it, and you will be able to find your way around a law library with confidence. You will know how to distinguish between the resources that contain the law itself (**primary authority**), those that summarize, analyze and describe it (**secondary authority**), and those that help you find the resources you need (**finding tools**). And, you will be able to assess how authoritative each resource is: is it something a court might rely on in deciding a case, or merely helpful to you in learning and understanding the area of law you are researching?

Of course, not every legal question has a definitive answer. For example, if you are asked whether it is legal to terminate an employee based upon his or her age, you will find that it depends upon the circumstances, including the age of the employee and requirements of the job. In fact, the short answer to many legal questions is, "it depends." But, if you know how to find and analyze the available resources, you will be able to describe the factors that determine the answer, and to make arguments both for and against a particular position.

Once you have found the resources that address your legal question, you must be able to cite them correctly for others. This book will tell you how to accurately cite the resources typically used in North Carolina, according to *The Bluebook: A Uniform System of Citation* (Columbia Law Review Ass'n et al. eds., 18th ed. 2005). Although in practice you may often shortcut the rules set out in *The Bluebook*, it is extremely helpful to know them. Maybe you will be lucky enough to work on a brief going to the Supreme Court, or perhaps you will need to figure out how to cite an obscure reference. If you know how to use *The Bluebook*, you can accurately cite virtually all legal resources, and make sense of any citations you encounter.

Research and citation may seem challenging at first. But, as with most skills, the more you practice, the better you will become.

Legal Research
in
North Carolina

Chapter 1

Background

Goals of Legal Research

Some legal professionals spend their entire careers researching and writing about legal questions. Others rarely set foot in a library. Either way, it is important that all legal professionals be equipped to find the answers to basic legal questions that may arise in a legal practice, whether contained in statutes, cases, or secondary sources.

In order to research effectively, you should know:

- the **legal bibliography**, i.e., where to find the various source materials for the law, including books and electronic information;
- how to **search** the legal bibliography efficiently to answer the questions at hand;
- how to **analyze** what you find and apply it to a particular situation;
- how to **write** down what you have found and what it means in a logically organized manner; and
- how to **cite** each resource you use so that your reader can find it without difficulty.

Sources of Law — Primary Authority

You cannot research the law effectively without a fundamental understanding of what it is. There are many meanings of the word, "law." One such meaning is a single statute—or rule—of a state or country which directs you to act, or refrain from acting, in a particular way. For example, consider the requirement that you drive slowly in a school zone, or register in order to be able to vote, or that you refrain from buying alcohol until you reach a certain age. Each of these requirements is derived from a law.

But, **the law** encompasses far more than a single statute. **The law** is a system or collection of principles and regulations established by some authority in a community, and applicable to its people. The authority that creates those principles and regulations is often referred to as a "jurisdiction." It might be local (e.g., a city or county), state (e.g., the State of North Carolina or the State of Tennessee), or federal (the United States).

In the United States, within each jurisdiction, the law emanates from a written constitution and from any of the three branches of government authorized by the constitution: the legislative branch, the judicial branch, and the executive branch. Constitutions set out the system of fundamental principles of law governing the state or country. They are broad, overarching documents, creating each branch of government, and outlining its powers and duties. They tend to be far more stable than statutes because they are not easily changed. North Carolina has its own constitution, and of course, the federal government has the United States Constitution. The state and federal Constitutions are often overlooked by researchers but contain some of the most important provisions of the law.

Whether it comes from the constitution itself, or one of the three branches of government, the law is **primary authority.** Examples of primary authority include constitutions, statutes, regulations, ordinances, court opinions, administrative agency opinions, treaties and executive orders.

Legislative Branch

The legislative branch of government is the place most people think of as the source of law. State and federal legislatures meet on a regular basis, consider new laws and changes to existing laws, and adopt those found to be appropriate after debate and discussion. The laws adopted by a legislature are typically called "statutes," and cover a wide variety of subject areas from crime to corporations to real property, and much, much more.

At the federal level, the legislature is known as the United States Congress. It consists of two chambers: the Senate and the House of Representatives. Together, these two chambers pass federal statutes called "public laws" that apply to everyone in the country. Federal statutes typically address issues of national importance, such as taxes, drug safety, banking, crime, interstate commerce, and the national defense, to name just a few. Congress can also pass "private laws" that apply to only one person or a group of people, such as a law granting citizenship to someone who otherwise would not be entitled to it.

State legislatures are known by a variety of official names, depending upon the state in question. In North Carolina, the state legislature in known as the North Carolina General Assembly. Like the federal Congress, it consists of two chambers: the Senate and the House of Representatives. The North Carolina General Assembly creates public and private laws known as statutes that govern the citizens of North Carolina, and in some cases, non-citizens who come within the state's borders. State laws address issues of statewide importance, such as divorce, property law, occupational licensing, inheritance, and the conduct of business transactions in the state.

There is even a legislative body at the local level. Most cities and counties have city councils and county commissions, or like bodies, which adopt laws applying to that locality. These laws typically are known as ordinances. A researcher working on a local issue such as zoning would want to become familiar with the city zoning code.

Remember that laws passed by legislative bodies, whether statutes or ordinances, are *primary authority*—they are the law itself and must be followed by those to whom the laws apply. Public laws are designed to have general application to all the citizens of the jurisdiction, whether the city, county, state, or country.

Legislatively created laws are typically compiled by subject matter into books called "codes" that are readily accessible to the citizens of the state. There are three commonly-used published versions of the federal statutes. The United States Code (U.S.C.) is the official publication of federal statutes by the United States government. The United States Code Annotated (U.S.C.A.) and the United States Code Service (U.S.C.S.) are unofficial versions of the Code published by two private companies—The West Group and LexisNexis(tm). All three publications contain the same laws in the same order with the same numbering system. Which version you use is a matter of preference based upon other features of the version. (See Chpt. 3 for more information).

Similarly, there are two published versions of the North Carolina statutes: the official North Carolina General Statutes published by LexisNexis, and the unofficial North Carolina General Statutes Annotated, published by The West Group.

Judicial Branch

The judicial branch of government is the system of courts in a particular jurisdiction. One function of the judicial branch is to interpret the laws created by the legislative branch of government.

The **federal courts** are authorized by the United States Constitution, Article III, Section 1:

> The judicial power of the United States shall be vested in one Supreme Court and in such inferior courts as Congress may from time-to-time ordain and establish.

Only the United States Supreme Court is specifically mentioned in the U.S. Constitution. All the other federal courts now in existence were created by Acts of Congress. The first such Act, the Judiciary Act of 1789, set the framework for the federal court system as it is today: trial courts known as "district" courts, intermediate "circuit" courts of appeal, and the Supreme Court.

Courts in the Federal Judiciary

United States Supreme Court—highest court in the nation

United States Courts of Appeal—intermediate appellate courts

United States District Courts—federal trial courts

The federal courts can hear only two categories of cases: those involving a "federal question" and those involving parties with a "diversity of citizenship." Cases involving a "federal question" are those wherein the court must interpret a federal law, treaty, or the U.S. Constitution. Of course, given the breadth of federal law, including the Constitution, a wide range of issues will be heard in the federal courts based upon a federal question. Cases in the "diversity of citizenship" category generally involve disputes between persons (including companies) of two or more different states where the "amount in controversy" exceeds $75,000.00, as set out in Title 28 of the United States Code, section 1332.[1]

Similarly, the **North Carolina court system** was also created by constitution. Article IV, § 1, of the North Carolina Constitution provides that the judicial power of the State is vested in a General Court of Justice (and a Court for the Trial of Impeachments). Article IV further provides for both a Superior Court and District Court Division (trial courts), and for an Appellate Division consisting of the North Carolina Supreme Court and the North Carolina Court of Appeals.[2]

Courts in the State Judiciary

North Carolina Supreme Court—highest court in the state

North Carolina Court of Appeals—intermediate appellate court

North Carolina Superior Court, District Court, Magistrates Court—
state trial courts

North Carolina courts hear cases involving questions of state law, and the North Carolina constitution. For civil cases, the amount in controversy dictates in which trial court the parties' case will be heard. The proper trial court for hearing criminal cases depends on the nature of the crime.

Occasionally, a case will involve issues which can be heard by both the state and federal court systems, for example when a person's misconduct violates both state and federal laws. In such cases, the state and federal courts have "concurrent jurisdiction." Such cases may be brought in either the state or federal courts.

Whether a court is state or federal, it creates "law" by deciding disputes between specific parties and making a written decision. Such decisions, also known as "opinions," describe the circumstances that led to the dispute, the existing law affecting that dispute, and the reasons for the court's decision. Many of these written opinions are published, particularly those written by appellate courts, and constitute a vast body of law known as "case law" or "common law." Like statutes, case law is also *primary authority*.

Cases sometimes involve the interpretation of a state or federal statute. However, there are many cases where no written statute governs the dispute. In such circum-

---

1. 28 U.S.C. § 1332 (2000).
2. N.C. Const. Art. IV, §§ 2, 5.

stances, the court must rely on previous cases of a similar nature, and, in general, attempt to decide the present case in accordance with the law set down in those earlier cases. In so doing, courts are guided by a doctrine known as *stare decisis*. Under *stare decisis*, rules or principles of law on which a court decided an earlier case are authoritative in all similar future cases arising in the same court or a lower court in the same jurisdiction. (See Chpt. 7.)

You can read the opinions of federal courts, and the appellate decisions of the North Carolina courts, in various series of books called *reporters*.

Executive Branch

The Executive Branch of government includes the president (or governor) and many of the administrative agencies of the government. The Executive Branch is charged with the administration and enforcement of the law. Even so, it can also be a source of law.

Consider all of the administrative agencies that affect your day-to-day life. On the federal level, the FDA mandates the nutrition labels on the food you buy at the store, the FAA creates airline safety regulations, and the EPA regulates the environment. Similarly, at the state level, the Building Code Council regulates construction methods, the Medical Board prohibits unlicensed physicians from practicing in North Carolina, and the Secretary of State's office makes rules affecting the sale of securities. Most of these mandates are made in the form of rules or regulations, and are primary authority.

In addition, agencies hear cases involving disputes over agency rules, and violations of those rules. Agency decisions are like court decisions, but they generally come from the executive branch. They too are primary authority.

The executive branch also makes law in less noticeable ways. For example, the executive branch of the federal government from time to time enters into treaties with other countries (with the advice and consent of the Senate). These treaties are law. In addition, both the President of the United States and the Governor of North Carolina have the authority to issue "executive orders" to regulate administrative agencies and government officials. These orders are also law.

References about the Law —
Secondary Authority

"Secondary authority" is anything that is not the law itself but that explains or comments on the law. Although it does not have the force of law, courts can rely on secondary authority when making a decision. Secondary authority can be very persuasive, depending upon the source. Examples of secondary authorities that are generally persuasive to the courts include:

- legal encyclopedias such as *American Jurisprudence* ("Am. Jur.") and *Corpus Juris Secundum* ("C.J.S.");
- legal dictionaries such as *Black's Law Dictionary*;
- annotations such as *American Law Reports* (A.L.R.);
- legal periodicals such as law reviews and bar journals;
- treatises and "hornbooks"; and
- "restatements" of the law on a particular subject (such as the *Restatement of the Law of Contracts* compiled by the American Law Institute).

What use is a secondary authority if it is not as persuasive as the primary authority? Why not go straight to the law itself? Sometimes, the sheer volume of primary authority available is daunting. If you are unfamiliar with the topic, you need a mechanism for focusing your search. Secondary authority can help. Often, it is a useful starting point.

Assume, for example, that you are asked to write a memorandum on employment discrimination. If you go straight to primary authorities, you will find numerous laws and cases on the subject covering various facts and legal issues. A secondary authority, such as a book on employment law, might be a good place to get some background information and hone in on the points of law you need to review. It will also increase your understanding of the subject area.

In addition, most secondary sources are excellent "finding tools," that is, they often contain cross references to other authorities, both primary and secondary, that will be useful in your research. Thus, you can often shortcut your research by starting with a good secondary authority and letting its author do some of your groundwork for you.

Secondary authorities are also helpful when you have read the law itself, but have questions as to its application. Secondary sources often describe how the law has been interpreted in various fact situations.

And, there will be times when there is no primary authority on point. In those cases, you may have to rely on a secondary authority to learn what the experts and commentators in the field think the law should be, and the arguments on both sides of an issue.

Getting to the Law and Other Legal References — Finding Tools

It is impossible for an ordinary person to know all the state statutes by heart, or in which of the hundreds of volumes of reporters a particular case is located. In order to find the law, and secondary sources about the law, finding tools are the key.

Finding tools are research books and materials that tell you where to find the law on a particular topic. That topic might be quite general, e.g., "employment law," or very specific, e.g., "employment discrimination based upon age — airline pilot." Some finding tools are nothing but large indexes to the law. For instance, both the United States Code and the North Carolina General Statutes have their own index volumes. In the case of the official U.S. Code, the general index itself takes up six volumes, while the official N.C. General Statutes Index is two volumes. These indexes are finding tools.

One popular finding tool, *Shepard's Citations*, contains no words, just coded series of numbers and letters. Once you understand how to translate the code, you can access primary and secondary authorities on any topic covered by a case, statute, or regulation.

Some legal resources include primary authority and finding tools. In a statute book, for instance, the statutes themselves are primary authority. They are followed by annotations and cross-references to other laws and cases interpreting the law. These are finding tools. The finding tools will often include references to secondary authorities too, such as law review articles.

There are even books which attempt to encompass primary authority, secondary authority, and finding tools, all in one place. These resources are known as "loose-leaf" services. They are typically limited to one subject area, for example antitrust law, employment law, or tax law. Within the loose-leaf volumes you will find statutes, cases, regulations, overviews, and commentary, with indexes to what's in the loose-leaf, and cross-references to outside sources of even more information.

The Weight of Authority

As should now be clear, both primary and secondary authority have utility. But when it is time to convince a court that your client's position is the correct one, the weight of authority you choose to put before the judge is critical.

In general, the most persuasive authority is primary. After all, primary law is the law itself, not merely an expert or commentator discussing the law. However, just because an authority is "primary" doesn't mean that a court must follow it. It depends upon how closely "on point" that authority is, and from what source it comes.

Suppose you are asked to determine how much notice is required to evict a tenant from an apartment.

- If you go to the North Carolina General Statutes book and find a law on the subject, that law is *primary authority* and it is very *persuasive*.
- If you instead read a learned treatise about landlord/tenant law in North Carolina written by a law professor who specializes in property law, that book is *secondary authority*, but is still very *persuasive*.
- If you instead go to an internet site created by a disgruntled former tenant who gives free advice to other tenants about how to keep from being evicted, any information you obtain will arguably be from a "secondary authority," but it will not be persuasive, particularly to a judge.

Mandatory Authority

Mandatory authority is an authority that a court is compelled to follow in deciding a case. Only primary authority can be mandatory. At best, secondary authority may be persuasive. A court typically must follow the dictates of an applicable statute or prior case on an issue. A court is never required to follow the suggestions of a law professor, encyclopedia or treatise about what the law is or should be.

In determining whether a primary authority is mandatory, or merely persuasive, it is helpful to keep in mind the relative status or rank of legislation and opinions. The highest form of legal authority is the Constitution. Statutes carry more authority than administrative rules or regulations. Thus, if there is a conflict between the text of a statute and a Constitutional provision, the Constitution will prevail. Likewise, if there is a conflict between the provisions of a rule and a statute, the statute will prevail. Parties often dispute whether they fall within the purview of a particular law or rule. The courts will then sort out whether a statute or rule applies, and whether it is unconstitutional or otherwise improper.

The highest ranking court opinions are those that come from the Supreme Court in any given jurisdiction. Thus, Supreme Court cases are binding on the Courts of Appeals, and the Courts of Appeals' decisions control over trial courts' decisions.

But, primary authority is not always mandatory. It is mandatory only if it is applicable in the jurisdiction, on point, and not in conflict with a higher authority. For example, North Carolina courts are not required to follow the laws of New Jersey, even if they would seem to address a particular situation.

Persuasive Authority

Persuasive authority is any authority that is not mandatory, but that still has relevance. It may not be directly on point, but applicable by analogy. Or, it may come from a source that the court is not bound to follow. Even so, persuasive authorities may be useful from time to time, especially when there isn't enough mandatory authority to address the issues at hand.

When is primary authority "mandatory" and when is it merely "persuasive?"

Assume that your law firm is considering whether to represent a family who was injured when the deck of the beach cottage they rented for a week collapsed under their weight. The facts demonstrate that the deck was old, had not been maintained, and rotted over time. A North Carolina statute makes the owner of vacation rental property liable for damages if the owner fails to maintain the property in fit and habitable condition.

The statute in this example is "on point" and applicable in North Carolina. Assuming this law does not conflict with any higher law, such as a provision of the NC Constitution, it is **mandatory authority** and the court must follow it.

Suppose, however, that there is no statute on the subject of **vacation** rental properties, but instead, a statute that addresses long-term **residential** rentals. Now you must carefully review the statute to see if it applies in a short-term vacation situation. If not, the statute might be persuasive, but it is certainly not mandatory.

Now assume that your case is before the NC Court of Appeals, there is only the residential rental statute on the books and the NC Supreme Court ruled in a previous case that the residential rental statute does not apply to vacation rentals. Here, no matter how persuasive the statute might appear, the Supreme Court's opinion is mandatory authority, and the Court of Appeals must follow it.

Organization of a Typical Lawbook

Whether you are researching in primary or secondary authority, mandatory or persuasive, the books you are using will be organized in similar ways. Once you have worked with a few standard resources, you will be able to figure out how to use others you have never seen. Too, if you know how books are typically arranged, you can often find shortcuts and alternatives to finding elusive but important information.

The law is literally "voluminous," that is, most legal resources are so large as to encompass many volumes. The **spine** of the book will typically indicate its name, and the volume number of the book. The volume number will help you pinpoint the information you seek, and also will be important when you do your citations. Likewise, important information pertaining to citation can usually be found on the **outside and inside covers** of the book, including the official title of the book, its publisher, edition and copyright information.

Toward the front of most law books you will find **Tables of Contents**, sometimes in both short and comprehensive form. When your use of an index leads you to a place in the book that is close to what you are looking for, but not exactly right, the tables of contents will often help you get to exactly the right place. You may also find a *Table of Cases* and *Table of Statutes* cited in the book to lead you to particular statutes and cases cited within.

In some books you will also find toward the front a **list of abbreviations** used in the book, and you may also find **instructions on "how to use this book."** This is especially true for loose-leafs and highly technical books like *Shepard's Citations*. Review these instructions when you are having difficulty getting around in the books using the usual methods.

Near the end of the book you may find an **index**. It is more likely, however, that the index will be in a separate volume or volumes. Indices are typically located at the far end of the set of books they reference.

You probably will find a flap built into the back cover of the book. Unless the book is very new, a **"pocket part" or "supplement"** will be inserted into the flap. These supplements are usually annual, and are designed to update the original text and add new developments in the law after the date the book was published. Thus, in order to get a complete picture of any given point of law, it is important to read both the main volume and its supplement.

Exercise 1 — Review Questions

1. Identify the three branches of government and give an example of the type of law each creates.

2. Identify whether each of the following is *primary authority ("P"), secondary authority ("S"),* or a *finding tool ("FT")*.

   A. A statute outlawing bribery. _____

   B. Case notes following the statute outlawing bribery, identifying cases where the court has addressed the elements of the crime. _____

   C. An index to the statutes. _____

   D. A hornbook about criminal law written by a law professor. _____

   E. A court opinion finding that the defendant assaulted the plaintiff. _____

   F. A regulation of the North Carolina State Bar prohibiting paralegals from drafting wills. _____

   G. A legal dictionary. _____

   H. A *Restatement of the Law of Torts*. _____

3. Assume that a federal statute outlaws public speeches, but the 1st Amendment to the U.S. Constitution provides for freedom of speech. If these two sources of law cannot be reconciled, which one prevails?

4. What are the federal trial courts called?

5. What are the state trial courts called?

6. If the North Carolina Court of Appeals rules one way on a question of law and the North Carolina Supreme Court rules the opposite, which court's opinion controls future cases? Does it matter whose opinion was written first?

7. Is secondary authority ever mandatory?

8. Is primary authority always mandatory?

Chapter 2

Introduction to Legal Citation and *The Bluebook*

When writing about the law, you must communicate the source of any information you find by citing it in a way your reader can understand. Good citation form allows your reader to understand and find the sources you have relied upon as part of your research.

Ideally, the citation of your source material won't take up so much room that it overwhelms the substance of your text, but will still clearly identify the books and materials you used. To shortcut the process in a way that all legal professionals can understand, the editors of the Columbia, Harvard, University of Pennsylvania, and Yale law reviews or journals have developed *The Bluebook: A Uniform System of Citation* (Columbia Law Review Ass'n et al. eds., 18th ed. 2005). Most lawyers follow the directives of *The Bluebook*, albeit loosely except on formal occasions.

The Bluebook contains rules of citation for virtually every kind of legal authority available, including statutes, cases, constitutions, administrative rules, books, magazines, law reviews, and looseleaf services.

Caveat on Using *The Bluebook*: Local Rules

Some courts have developed their own rules about how certain authorities should be cited. When preparing a document for any court, you should always check first to determine if there are any court rules concerning citation, format or any other matter affecting your submission. **Where the court's rules differ from those of *The Bluebook*, follow the rules of the court to which you will submit your document.**

Structure of *The Bluebooook*

The Bluebook is organized in four parts:

1. practitioners' rules on blue paper at the front of the book (for those in private practice as opposed to academics),
2. general rules of citation that apply to all sorts of authorities,
3. rules for citing particular types of authorities, like statutes, cases and books, and
4. tables at the back of the book, on blue-edged paper, that help you choose the proper authority and abbreviate correctly.

The Bluepages

The Bluebook is written primarily for scholars writing for academic journals and law reviews. Unless you are working in an academic setting, you will have to modify *The Bluebook's* general rules in accordance with its *Bluepages*, found on the blue pages at the front. Theoretically, the *Bluepages* simplify the rules in the main body of the text, and the tables in the back. However, their presence often means that you must look in at least two places in *The Bluebook* to determine how to cite any resource correctly.

Even so, the *Bluepages* generally provide a clear template for basic citation forms used by lawyers in private practice and other legal professionals. They include tips on how to integrate a cite into legal writing (B1 and B2), the elements of a citation (B3), introductory signals (B4), and then basic rules of citation for various authorities, including cases (B5), statutes and rules (B6), constitutions (B7), books (B8), journals (B9), and court documents (B10).

Rule B13 addresses typeface conventions. In general, practitioners use only ordinary roman type, and either underscoring or italics. Those authorities which should be underscored or italicized are listed, and include case names, book titles, and introductory signals.[1]

When you are reading the rules in the **main body** of *The Bluebook*, you will often see text that includes both large and small caps. For example, a rule governing citation of a statute might look like this: DEL. CODE ANN. § 96-1005 (Supp. 1998). Or, a rule concerning citation of a book might contain a citation like: CHARLES DICKENS, BLEAK HOUSE 50 (Norman Page ed., Penguin Books 1971) (1853). Notice the type style in each of the two citations. It includes both large and small capital letters. You will see this style throughout *The Bluebook*. However, as required by the *Bluepages*, you must convert the type in these examples (and your own citations) to ordinary type.

DEL. CODE ANN. § 96-1005 (Supp. 1998) becomes:

---

1. *The Bluebook: A Uniform System of Citation* B13, at 23–24 (Columbia Law Review Ass'n et al. eds., 18th ed. 2005).

Del. Code Ann. § 96-1005 (Supp. 1998).

CHARLES DICKENS, BLEAK HOUSE 50 (Norman Page ed., Penguin Books 1971) (1853) becomes:
Charles Dickens, <u>Bleak House</u> 50 (Norman Page ed., Penguin Books 1971) (1853)

In the example of the Charles Dickens book, not only did the type change from large and small caps to ordinary type, but also the name of the book, "Bleak House," was underlined as required by B13 in *Bluepages*. Italics are also permissible. Thus, as a practitioner you could cite "Bleak House" correctly either of two ways:

- Charles Dickens, <u>Bleak House</u> 50 (Norman Page ed., Penguin Books 1971)
- Charles Dickens, *Bleak House* 50 (Norman Page ed., Penguin Books 1971).

Section B2 describes how to integrate your citations into written documents as either a citation sentence, or a citation clause. For example, assume you are writing a memo to the senior partner of your law firm. Rule B2 allows you to include the citation within the text of a sentence, or to make the citation its own "sentence." Here is a case citation that is included as a clause within the text of a sentence:

In <u>Still v. Lance</u>, 279 N.C. 254, 182 S.E.2d 403 (1971), this Court ruled that employees without a definite term of employment ordinarily may be fired without grounds.

Here, the same idea is expressed, but the citation is its own separate sentence:

This Court has previously ruled that employees without a definite term of employment ordinarily may be fired without grounds. <u>Still v. Lance</u>, 279 N.C. 254, 182 S.E.2d 403 (1971).

Note that in the second example, the citation concludes with a period, just as an ordinary textual sentence would. Many of the examples you will see in *The Bluebook* will likewise end with a period. Whether you include that period in your citation depends upon whether your cite is a stand-alone sentence (include the period), or part of a textual sentence (don't include the period unless your cite ends the sentence).

Other matters addressed in the *Bluepages* include parallel case citations, short forms of citations, capitalization in court documents and legal memoranda, and other details. These will be addressed throughout this book in the context of the authority being cited.

General Rules of Citation — *Bluebook* Rules 1–9

Rules 1 through 9 are general rules of citation that apply to many authorities. Much of what is contained within these rules is more important to law review authors than to practitioners. However, from time to time, some of these rules must be consulted.

For example, Rule 3 deals with citations including **volume numbers, parts, and supplements**, as well as **section, paragraph and page numbers**. These are common in citations to statutes, books, and looseleaf services.

Rule 4 is also important for practitioners. It gives a variety of **short forms of citations** that you can use in a memo or brief, once you have given the citation in full to a particular authority. Knowing how to properly shortcut your citation form makes it easier to type legal documents, saves space, and makes for easier reading.

For rules on **quoting** other sources, look to Rule 5. (See Chapter 12.)

Rule 6 on abbreviations, numerals and symbols and Rule 8 on capitalization can be important and will be addressed in the context of cases, law review articles, and other secondary authorities.

Rules of Citation for Specific Legal Resources — *Bluebook* Rules 10–21

In Rules 10 through 21, *The Bluebook* gives specific instruction on how to cite virtually every type of legal authority, whether common or rare. Unlike Rules 1 through 9 which apply to a variety of authorities, Rules 10 through 21 each apply to a particular type of authority. For example, Rule 10 is about cases, Rule 11 is about constitutions, and Rule 12 is about statutes. These three rules are among the most important, as they concern the most widely used primary authorities.

The Bluebook also addresses citation of other primary authorities including administrative rules and executive materials (Rule 14) and important secondary authorities such as books (Rule 15), periodicals (Rule 16), and looseleaf services (Rule 19). There are also rules devoted to foreign and international materials (Rules 20 and 21).

Many legal resources are now available online or through other electronic media. *The Bluebook* gives specific direction on how to cite sources that are available in both book and digital form, or that are available exclusively through electronic media (Rule 18).

Tables

Nearly half the pages of *The Bluebook* are tables in the back of the book. All the tables are printed on blue-bordered paper. As explained in *The Bluebook's* introduction, "The tables show, among other things, which authority to cite and how to abbreviate properly. Individual tables are referenced throughout the book."[2]

---

2. *Id.*, at 1.

For many citations, the most important table is the first ("T.1"). It deals with "United States Jurisdictions." This includes abbreviations and citation formulas for a variety of federal and state authorities. Federal authorities covered in Table T.1 include:

- the United States Supreme Court,
- other federal courts including the courts of appeal and district courts,
- federal statutory compilations such as the U.S. Code,
- federal session laws, and
- federal administrative regulations.

Each state is separately addressed in T.1 in alphabetical order. Within each state, entries can be found for that state's:

- appellate courts
- statutory compilation,
- session laws, and
- administrative compilation.

Look in your *Bluebook's Table T.1* and find the entry for North Carolina. You may find it helpful to tab the page on which it begins. Immediately under the title "North Carolina (NC)" you will see a Web address: http://www.nccourts. org. This is the address for North Carolina's Administrative Office of the Courts. You can find a variety of legal information online at this address, including appellate opinions from the North Carolina Supreme Court and Court of Appeals.

The North Carolina section of T.1 is laid out much like each of the other states' entries. It begins with the highest court in our state, the Supreme Court. As shown in the table, in a case citation, the appropriate abbreviation for the North Carolina Supreme Court is "N.C." — just as it appears in the parentheses immediately following the bold catchline, "Supreme Court." Listed under the entry for the North Carolina Supreme Court are all the *reporters* in which the N.C. Supreme Court opinions have been published since the Court's inception, the dates the cases were reported in each one, and the appropriate abbreviation for each reporter. Unless the case is very old, you will cite the *North Carolina Reports* ("N.C.") and/or the *South Eastern Reporter* ("S.E." or "S.E.2d").

Next you will find an entry for the North Carolina Court of Appeals ("N.C. Ct. App.") and the appropriate abbreviation for the two reporters in which Court of Appeals cases appear ("N.C. App." and "S.E." or "S.E.2d"). (See Chpt. 6 for more information on citing cases.)

After the entries for the NC appellate courts you will see the entry for North Carolina's official statutory compilation, known as the "North Carolina General Statutes." According to Table T.1, the North Carolina General Statutes are abbreviated in a citation to: "N.C. Gen. Stat. § x-x (year)." The "x-x" stands for a section number, and the "year" is for the year the statute book was published. (See Chpt. 4 for more information on citing statutes.) Immediately following is the entry for the unofficial West publication of the North Carolina General Statutes.

Finally, at the end of the North Carolina sections are the entries for North Carolina's administrative code and the *North Carolina Register*. These deal with state agency rules and actions. (See Chpt. 8 for more information on citing agency rules.)

Finding Your Way around *The Bluebook*

The Bluebook has various finding tools to help you locate the necessary rules to properly cite a particular resource. One such tool is the use of different colored pages; white in the middle for the substantive rules, blue at the front for the practitioners' rules, and blue borders at the back for tables.

At the very back of *The Bluebook*, on white pages, you will find an alphabetized index to the rules, *Bluepages* and tables. Included in the index are entries for particular legal resources, and for particular citation issues. For example, if you have to cite a case to the Court of Military Appeals, you can simply look in the index under "c" for "court" or "m" for "military" and find the appropriate reference to the page in *The Bluebook* that tells you how to cite such cases. Or, if you are trying to remember how to cite something that appears in a supplement, simply look under "s" in the index. "Page references in black are to INSTRUCTIONS; page references in blue are to EXAMPLES."[3]

In addition, if you know generally the section of *The Bluebook* you need, you can use its back cover to find your way quickly to the rule. Each of the main topics of the book are listed there, beginning with the Introduction and ending with the Index. The white numbers refer to the page on which the particular topic appears; the medium blue to the rule or table number.

Finally, if you simply leaf through *The Bluebook*, you will find that the particular rule being addressed is identified in bold on the outside edge of the page at the beginning of the text about that rule.

Quick References

On the inside covers and facing pages of *The Bluebook*, you will find two extra tables that can shortcut your search for the appropriate *Bluebook* rule. The table on the front cover is for law review authors, but the one on the back is for practitioners. This back table includes examples of citations to commonly used legal resources, set out in the practitioners' form and style. Although not comprehensive, you can use it for guidance in ordinary citations.

---

3. Id. at 381.

Exercise 2 — Using *The Bluebook*

1. Go to the back cover of *The Bluebook* and find R 1–9: General Rules of Citation and Style.

    A. On what page does that section begin?

    B. What is the title of rule R3?

    C. On what page does rule R3 begin?

    D. Look on the outer edges of the pages in *The Bluebook* and find Rule 8. On what page does it begin, and what is it about?

2. As a practitioner, if you want a quick reference for a case citation, where would you look? What is the name of the first case listed there? (Give the parties names exactly as they appear in the example, including punctuation and underlining.)

3. If you are working on a brief that will be submitted to a court on behalf of a client, must you follow the *Bluepages* in *The Bluebook*?

4. Convert the following citation to a book so that it comports with the *Bluepages*: HAROLD W. FUSON, JR., TELLING IT ALL: A LEGAL GUIDE TO THE EXERCISE OF FREE SPEECH 57–58 (1995).

5. Convert the following citation to a North Carolina General Statute so that it comports with the *Bluepages*: N.C. GEN. STAT. § 150B-39 (2004).

6. Go to Table T.1 in *The Bluebook* and find the section labeled, "United States Jurisdictions." For each abbreviation given, make your spacing exact.

    A. What is the abbreviation for the United States Supreme Court?

    B. What is the abbreviation for the *United States Reports* for the years 1875 forward?

    C. What is the abbreviation for the *Supreme Court Reporter*? (Make sure your spacing is exact.)

D. What is the abbreviation for the *Lawyer's Edition*? What is the abbreviation for the *Lawyer's Edition, second series*?

E. What is the abbreviation for *Federal Reporter*, second series?

F. In which reporter would a case from the United States Court of Appeals be found?

G. In which reporter should you cite a recent case from the United States District Court, if possible? How do you know?

H. What does the abbreviation "D. Mass." mean that appears after the entry for **District Courts** in T.1, page 195? What does the entry "S.D.N.Y." mean? Note the difference in spacing in the two examples given.

7. Go to the North Carolina entry in T.1.

A. What page is it on?

B. What is the abbreviation for the North Carolina Supreme Court?

C. What is the abbreviation for the two reporters from which recent North Carolina Supreme Court should be cited?

D. What is the abbreviation for the North Carolina Court of Appeals?

E. What is the abbreviation for the two reporters in which recent North Carolina Court of Appeals opinions should be cited? (Make your spacing exact.)

F. What is the citation form for the preferred source from which North Carolina statutes should be cited? (Copy it exactly as it appears in the table.)

G. What is the name of the place where North Carolina administrative rules can be found?

Chapter 3

Constitutions and Statutes

You may begin a research project in a variety of legal resources. Where you begin depends upon the subject matter, its complexity, and your level of knowledge about it. In this book, you will start with constitutions and statutes. Both are primary authorities. Once you learn to use them, you will begin to understand how many other legal resources work. And, you may be fortunate enough to find a quick and definitive answer to your legal question.

Constitutions

Each state has its own constitution, as does the United States. North Carolina adopted its first state constitution in 1776. It has had two replacements since then; the current state constitution was created in 1971. The United States has had its Constitution since 1789. These constitutions set out the system of fundamental principles by which the country or state is governed.

Constitutions provide a framework on which the government and its subdivisions operate. They give power to the government to pass laws, but also set limits on that power to protect individual freedoms. In general, constitutions are not designed to deal with day to day issues of life, but rather, to set policy for how a government is to act. These policies are carried out by the legislature in the form of statutes.

CONTENTS OF THE NORTH CAROLINA CONSTITUTION:

Historical Perspective and Preamble

Article I: Declaration of Rights

Article II: Legislative

Article III: Executive

Article IV: Judicial

Article V: Finance

Article VI: Suffrage and Eligibility to Vote

Article VII: Local Government

Article VIII: Corporations

Article IX: Education

Article X: Homesteads and Exemptions

Article XI: Punishments, Corrections and Charities

Article XII: Military Forces

Article XIII: Conventions, Constitutional Amendment and Revision

Article XIV: Miscellaneous

Statutes

There are literally thousands of state and federal laws on the books. They address far-ranging issues including criminal misconduct, business operations and domestic issues. How did these laws come to be?

Creation and Publication of Statutes

Statutes are created through the legislative process. Ordinary citizens, lobbyists and others regularly present their ideas for new laws and amendments of existing laws to members of Congress or the state legislature. When a legislator likes the idea, he or she may draft a bill (or more likely, have a member of the legislative staff draft it based upon the legislator's directives). Once drafted, the idea becomes a proposed bill. Thereafter, it will be available for researchers in several forms.

1. *Bill.* First, the draft legislation is introduced into either the House of Representatives or the Senate. Once a bill has been introduced, it is published by the legislature and available to the public.

2. *Act.* If the bill passes both the House and Senate (and is not vetoed), it becomes law, that is, an Act. The first official publication of the Act is known as a *"slip law,"* and is available on a "slip" of paper (usually 8½ x 11), or in pamphlet form, from the legislature.

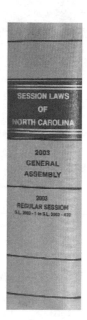

3. *Session Laws*. All of the Acts adopted by a particular session of a legislature are bound together and published in one large book, or set of books, called the "session laws." The session laws passed by the United States Congress are known as the *Statutes at Large*. The session laws passed by the North Carolina General Assembly are known as the *North Carolina Session Laws*.

A session of both the United States Congress and the North Carolina General Assembly lasts two years. The "regular session" of the North Carolina General Assembly is held in the odd numbered years; the "short session," involving limited subject matter, is held in the even-numbered years. Both the regular and short sessions are part of the same legislative term.

Statutes are arranged chronologically within each volume of session laws. Each volume has a subject index, but there is no master index covering all sessions. This makes it difficult to research current law using the session laws—to find a particular statute, you first have to know which year the statute was passed, then go the subject index for the session laws of that year and look it up. Using the session laws is not a realistic method of finding current statutes on a particular topic.

4. *Codes*. In order to simplify the process of finding all the statutes currently in force, both the state and federal governments have compiled their statutes into codes organized by the subject matter of the statutes they contain. A code includes all the public laws in effect in a particular jurisdiction, no matter when those laws were adopted. The official North Carolina code, known as the North Carolina General Statutes, takes up nineteen volumes of books (plus two index volumes), while the US Code takes far more.

Codes may be official or unofficial. Official codes are those authorized by the lawmakers, e.g. the North Carolina General Assembly or the United States Congress. Their topical arrangement and numbering system is determined by the government. Unofficial codes are published by private, for-profit companies. Unofficial codes contain the exact same laws as the official code, in the same order and using the same numbering system. The difference between the various codes for a particular jurisdiction lies in the additional information each publisher chooses to provide about the statutes it contains, such as case annotations and cross-references to related materials (see *Organization of Codes* below).

In the federal system, there are three widely-used publications of the code: the *United States Code* ("U.S.C."), the *United States Code Annotated* ("U.S.C.A."), and the *United States Code Service* ("U.S.C.S."). The U.S.C. is the official code, sanctioned by the United States government. The U.S.C.A. and U.S.C.S. are both privately published, U.S.C.A. by West Publishing Company and U.S.C.S. by Matthew Bender & Company, a member of the LexisNexis® Group. You can look up federal statutes in any of these publications.

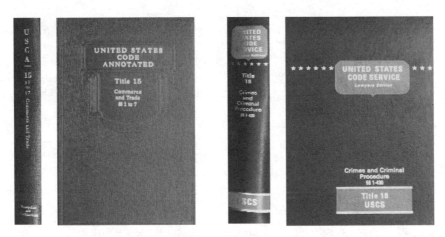

U.S.C.A. cover reprinted with the permission of West, a Thomson Business; U.S.C.S. cover reprinted with the permission of Matthew Bender & Company, Inc., a member of the Lexis-Nexis Group.

Although the U.S.C. is the official code, in practice you are more likely to use either the U.S.C.A. or U.S.C.S. Many legal professionals choose either the U.S.C.A. or U.S.C.S. because of the cross-references, historical information and case "annotations" the publisher includes in it. (Annotations are short summaries of the law and facts of cases interpreting the statute.) Both the U.S.C.A. and the U.S.C.S. contain a great deal of this kind of information about the statutes printed within them.

In North Carolina, the code is known as the North Carolina General Statutes, and it is published both officially and unofficially. The official code is published by LexisNexis®, Matthew Bender & Company, Inc. It is authorized by the North Carolina government to be the official compilation of the general statutes of the state. The unofficial code is published by the West Group and is called *West's North Carolina General Statutes Annotated*. Both sets of the statutes are annotated and contain a variety of information in addition to the statutes themselves. The cross-references in the two versions vary slightly, with the West version tending toward references to other West products as well as cases, and the official LexisNexis® version referencing primarily cases and law review articles. Because West has a vast library of legal resources, it is a viable alternative to the well-established and also popular official version of the statutes.

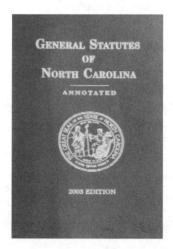 

North Carolina General Statutes cover reprinted with the permission of Matthew Bender & Company, Inc., a member of the LexisNexis Group; North Carolina General Statutes Annotated cover reprinted with the permission of West, a Thomson Business.

Organization of Codes

Using codes is the best way to find a current statute on a particular topic. As discussed above, codes are organized by subject matter, contain all the public laws in force in the jurisdiction, and are well indexed.

The United States Code is organized into fifty broad subject matter topics called "titles." When a new statute is passed, it is inserted into one of the existing 50 titles.

TITLES OF THE U.S. CODE	
1. General Provisions	26. Internal Revenue Code
2. The Congress	27. Intoxicating Liquors
3 The President	28. Judiciary and Judicial Procedure
4. Flag, Seal, Etc.	29. Labor
5. Government Employees	30. Mineral Lands and Mining
6. Official and Penal Bonds	31. Money and Finance
7. Agriculture	32. National Guard
8. Aliens and Nationality	33. Navigation and Navigable Waters
9. Arbitration	34. (Navy) (Now in Title 10)
10. Armed Forces	35. Patents
11. Bankruptcy	36 Patriotic Societies & Observances
12. Banks and Banking	37. Pay & Allowances of Uniformed Services
13. Census	38. Veterans' Benefits
14. Coast Guard	39. Postal Service
15. Commerce and Trade	40. Public Buildings, Property and Works
16. Conservation	41. Public Contracts
17. Copyrights	42. Public Health and Welfare
18. Crimes & Criminal Procedure	43. Public Lands
19. Customs Duties	44. Public Printings and Documents
20. Education	45. Railroads
21. Food and Drugs	46. Shipping
22. Foreign Relations	47. Telegraphs, Telephones & Radiotelegraphs
23. Highways	48. Territories and Insular Possessions
24. Hospitals, Asylums, Etc.	49. Transportation
25. Indians	50. War and National Defense

North Carolina's code, the "North Carolina General Statutes," contains over 200 chapters rather than titles. When a new general statute is passed, it is usually inserted into one of the existing chapters. However, from time to time, new chapters are created. When this happens, the new chapter is placed near other chapters on a similar subject matter. Thus, if a new chapter were to fit best between existing chapters 14 and 15, it would be denominated as 14A. And, if 14A already existed, the new chapter would be labeled 14B, and so on. Thus, the chapters of the North Carolina General Statutes are sometimes directly chronological, as in 13 to 14 to 15, and sometimes have lettered chapters squeezed between. For example, between Chapters 93 and 94 of the NC General Statutes are chapters 93A, 93B, 93C, 93D and 93E.

Chapters are often further subdivided. Pick up any volume of the North Carolina General Statutes and open it to the beginning of a chapter. In most cases, you will find a table of contents for each of the statutory provisions within the chapter. Look within the Table of Contents and you may also find that the chapter is subdivided into smaller parts called "articles," and that each article contains a number of different sections. Likewise, pick up any volume of the U.S. Code and open it to the beginning of a title. You will find that it too contains a table of contents, and that the title is divided into sub-parts called chapters. Each chapter contains a number of individual sections.

Figure 3.1 is an example of the beginning of a chapter in the official North Carolina General Statutes. Note that it begins with the chapter number (19) and topic (offenses against public morals), followed by a table of contents including each article and section of the chapter. Following the table of contents is the beginning of the first article, and the first section within it (section 19-1).

Chapter 19.

Offenses Against Public Morals.

ARTICLE 1.

Abatement of Nuisances.

§ 19-1. What are nuisances under this Chapter.

(a) The erection, establishment, continuance, maintenance, use, ownership or leasing of any building or place for the purpose of assignation, prostitution, gambling, illegal possession or sale of alcoholic beverages, illegal possession or sale of controlled substances as defined in the North Carolina Controlled Substances Act, or illegal possession or sale of obscene or lewd matter, as defined in this Chapter, shall constitute a nuisance.

(b) The erection, establishment, continuance, maintenance, use, ownership or leasing of any building or place wherein or whereon are carried on, conducted, or permitted repeated acts which create and constitute a breach of the peace shall constitute a nuisance.

(b1) The erection, establishment, continuance, maintenance, use, ownership or leasing of any building or place wherein or whereon are carried on, conducted, or permitted repeated activities or conditions which violate a local ordinance regulating sexually oriented businesses so as to contribute to adverse secondary impacts shall constitute a nuisance.

(c) The building, place, vehicle, or the ground itself, in or upon which a nuisance as defined in subsection (a), (b), or (b1) of this section is carried on, and the furniture, fixtures, and contents, are also declared a nuisance, and

123

Figure 3.1   Copyright 2003—Matthew Bender & Company, Inc., a member of the LexisNexis Group.

Within each title or chapter of a code, individual statutes are known as sections. To identify a particular statute in the U.S. Code, you must know both its title and section number. (You can find these in an index to the code, as more fully described below.) For example, if you are looking for the tax law dealing with your retirement account, you would need to know that it is addressed in Title 26 of the U.S. Code, section 401(k). Similarly, if you wanted to find the law that addresses the punishment for first degree murder in North Carolina, you would need to know that it is in chapter 14 of the General Statutes, section 17.

Now look at an individual statute (a section) from either the U.S. Code or the N.C. General Statutes such as North Carolina General Statute section 136-89.48 depicted in Figure 3.2. The statute set out in Figure 3.2 is part of Chapter 136 of the North Carolina General Statutes, Article 6D. At the beginning, the section number is printed in bold (§ 136-89.48), followed by a brief summary of the section's topic ("Declaration of Policy"). This topic heading is called a "catch-line." It is not part of the law itself, but merely a very brief summary of what the law is about.

Next is the text of the statute. Some statutes are quite short—even one sentence—like the one illustrated in Figure 3.2. Others may go on for pages. Longer statutes are generally subdivided into lettered and numbered subsections. For example, § 136-89.49, is divided into three such subsections.

Immediately after the text of the statute, you will find the date the statute was first enacted and the date of each subsequent amendment, or change, to the statute. Also included are cross references to the session laws where the statute and amendments first appeared. In the official North Carolina code, this information appears inside a parenthetical; in the unofficial code, it stands alone as a separate paragraph.

For example, look at the second statute in Figure 3.2, N.C. Gen. Stat. § 136-89.49 (2003). At the end of the text of the statute, before the "Case Notes" is a parenthetical phrase that says, "(1957, c. 993, s. 2; 1973, c. 507, s. 5; 1977, c. 464, s. 7.1)." This tells you that the statute was first enacted in 1957, and that you will find it **as it read when it was enacted** in chapter ("c.") 993, section ("s.") 2, of the 1957 North Carolina Session Laws. It also tells you that the statute was amended for the first time in 1973, and that the amendment can be found in chapter 507, section 5, of the 1973 session laws. The statute was next amended in 1977; that amendment is in the 1977 session laws, chapter 464, section 7.1. Subsequent dates and numbers will give you each of the subsequent amendments to the statute, in chronological order. The version of the text you see before you is the most current text of the law as it existed on the publication date of the book you are reading.

Following the text of the statute and the dates of enactment and amendment you will often find a series of finding tools, commonly referred to collectively as "annotations." They refer to other relevant legal resources. Annotations vary depending upon how often a statute is litigated, how long it has been in effect, and how controversial its subject matter.

Typical annotations in a statute book include:

ARTICLE 6C.

State Toll Bridges and Revenue Bonds.

§§ 136-89.31 through 136-89.47: Repealed by Session Laws 1977, c. 464, s. 22.

ARTICLE 6D.

Controlled-Access Facilities.

§ 136-89.48. Declaration of policy.

The General Assembly hereby finds, determines, and declares that this Article is necessary for the immediate preservation of the public peace, health and safety, the promotion of the general welfare, the improvement and development of transportation facilities in the State, the elimination of hazards at grade intersections, and other related purposes. (1957, c. 993, s. 1.)

CASE NOTES

Designating Highway as "Controlled-Access" Is Exercise of Police Power. — When the State Highway Commission (now Department of Transportation) acts in the interest of public safety, convenience and general welfare, in designating highways as controlled-access highways, its action is the exercise of the police power of the State. Wofford v. North Carolina State Hwy. Comm'n, 263 N.C. 677, 140 S.E.2d 376, cert. denied, 382 U.S. 822, 86 S. Ct. 50, 15 L. Ed. 2d 67 (1965).

Impairing Property Value by Exercise of Police Power Gives No Right to Compensation. — The impairment of the value of property by the exercise of police power, where property itself is not taken, does not entitle the owner to compensation. Wofford v. North Carolina State Hwy. Comm'n, 263 N.C. 677, 140 S.E.2d 376, cert. denied, 382 U.S. 822, 86 S. Ct. 50, 15 L. Ed. 2d 67 (1965).

Applied in Moses v. State Hwy. Comm'n, 261 N.C. 316, 134 S.E.2d 664 (1964).

Cited in Snow v. North Carolina State Hwy. Comm'n, 262 N.C. 169, 136 S.E.2d 678 (1964); Prestige Realty Co. v. State Hwy. Comm'n, 1 N.C. App. 82, 160 S.E.2d 83 (1968).

§ 136-89.49. Definitions.

When used in this Article:
  (1) "Department" means the Department of Transportation.
  (2) "Controlled-access facility" means a State highway, or section of State highway, especially designed for through traffic, and over, from or to which highway owners or occupants of abutting property, or others, shall have only a controlled right or easement of access.
  (3) "Frontage road" means a way, road or street which is auxiliary to and located on the side of another highway, road or street for service to abutting property and adjacent areas and for the control of access to such other highway, road or street. (1957, c. 993, s. 2; 1973, c. 507, s. 5; 1977, c. 464, s. 7.1.)

CASE NOTES

A **"controlled-access facility,"** as defined in this section, is a limited access highway where the State Highway Commission (now Department of Transportation) acquires the legal right to cut off entirely the abutting own-er's right of direct access to and from the highway on which his property abuts. Barnes v. North Carolina State Hwy. Comm'n, 257 N.C. 507, 126 S.E.2d 732 (1962).

"Frontage Road". — A road constructed by

138

- **cross-references** to related statutes,
- **historical and statutory notes** including information about the **effect of amendments** on the language of the statute over time and **Congressional or legislative intent** in enacting the statute,
- **opinions of the attorney general** on the meaning and effect of the statute,
- summaries of articles in law reviews, journals and other **legal periodicals** that discuss the statute in question,
- other **library references** to secondary sources such as encyclopedias (published by the same company as the publisher of the statute book you are using), and
- **case notes** summarizing appellate decisions that have interpreted the statute in question and listing additional cases that have cited the statute.

Supplements

Unless a statute book has been issued very recently, it will be supplemented with additional information that has become available since the date the statute book was published. This supplemental information is published in a separate soft-cover booklet called an "interim supplement," "pocket part," or "cumulative supplement." Often, these supplements fit inside a flap or "pocket" inside the back cover of the statute book, hence the term, "pocket part."

In order to be sure you are reading the most current version of the law in question, you must **check the supplement** or pocket part to find out if the statute has been amended since the publication date of the hard-cover book you are using. It is easy for an inexperienced researcher to forget to update his or her research by checking the supplement, but can be a critical error.

The annual supplements are cumulative: they contain all the changes that have been made to the statutes from the time the bound volume was published to the time the supplement was published. Each year, when the new annual supplement comes out, you can throw away the previous year's supplement. All the changes in the former supplement that are still valid will be included in the new supplement, along with any additional changes that have been made in the previous year.

As more statutes are changed over time, the supplements themselves can become quite thick. When that happens, the publisher typically will print a new bound volume, updating all the statutes within it so that they are current. Volumes including frequently amended statutes are more likely to be reprinted regularly. Volumes including less often amended statutes might not be reprinted for many years. In either case, however, you can usually determine the current version of any law by checking the main volume and its supplement. (It is possible for changes to be made after the supplement is published. Advance sheets showing these changes may be available.)

If you are working with the North Carolina General Statutes, it is important to know that the official version is currently being reprinted every two years. The first year of printing, there are only main volumes, and no supplements. The second year, supplements are added. In the hardbound version, the supplements are added as pocket parts. In the softbound version of the statutes, supplements are printed in two separate volumes and shelved at the end of the main volumes. Thus, if you do not find a pocket part in your volume of the official statutes, it may be because (1) there is no supplement; or (2) the supplement is in a separate volume.

When a North Carolina statute appears in the supplement, even if only one subsection is changed, the entire **section** is reprinted in full in the supplement. This is so even if the section is pages long and the change is to only one word. So, if the statute is in the supplement of the North Carolina General Statutes or West's North Carolina General Statutes Annotated, you need not look at its text in the main volume.

On the other hand, if you are working with the U.S. Code, whether U.S.C., U.S.C.A., or U.S.C.S., you will find that only the subsections of a statute that have been changed will appear in the supplement. The unchanged subsections will not. This means that in order to read one statute as it is currently written, you will have to read parts of it in the main volume and parts of it in the supplement.

18 USCS § 44   CRIMES & CRIMINAL PROCEDURE

L. 91-135, § 8, 83 Stat. 281) was repealed by Act Nov. 16, 1981, P. L. 97-79, § 9(b)(2), 95 Stat. 1079. The section provided for marking of packages or containers of wild creatures or parts and prescribed a penalty for false marking. Similar provisions are contained in 16 USCS §§ 3371 et seq.

[§ 45. Repealed]

HISTORY; ANCILLARY LAWS AND DIRECTIVES

This section (Act June 25, 1948, ch 645, § 1, 62 Stat. 688) was repealed by Act Nov. 29, 1990, P. L. 101-647, Title XII, § 1206(a), 104 Stat. 4832. The section provided for the capturing or killing of carrier pigeons.

§ 46. Transportation of water hyacinths

(a) Whoever knowingly delivers or receives for transportation, or transports, in interstate commerce, alligator grass (alternanthera philoxeroides), or water chestnut plants (trapa natans) or water hyacinth plants (eichhornia crassipes) or the seeds of such grass or plants; or

(b) Whoever knowingly sells, purchases, barters, exchanges, gives, or receives any grass, plant, or seed which has been transported in violation of subsection (a); or

(c) Whoever knowingly delivers or receives for transportation, or transports, in interstate commerce, an advertisement, to sell, purchase, barter, exchange, give, or receive alligator grass or water chestnut plants or water hyacinth plants or the seeds of such grass or plants—

Shall be fined not more than $500, or imprisoned not more than six months, or both.

(Added Aug. 1, 1956, ch 825, § 1, 70 Stat. 797.)

CROSS REFERENCES

This section is referred to in 18 USCS § 14.

§ 47. Use of aircraft or motor vehicles to hunt certain wild horses or burros; pollution of watering holes

(a) Whoever uses an aircraft or a motor vehicle to hunt, for the purpose of capturing or killing, any wild unbranded horse, mare, colt, or burro running at large on any of the public land or ranges shall be fined not more than $500, or imprisoned not more than six months, or both.

(b) Whoever pollutes or causes the pollution of any watering hole on any of the public land or ranges for the purpose of trapping, killing, wounding, or maiming any of the animals referred to in subsection (a) of this section shall be fined not more than $500, or imprisoned not more than six months, or both.

(c) As used in subsection (a) of this section—

Figure 3.3   Copyright 1993—Matthew Bender & Company, Inc., a member of the LexisNexis Group.

18 USCS § 43   CRIMES & CRIMINAL PROCEDURE

(4) Death. Any person who, in the course of a violation of subsection (a), causes the death of an individual shall be fined under this title and imprisoned for life or for any term of years.

(c) **Restitution.** An order of restitution under section 3663 or 3663A of this title with respect to a violation of this section may also include restitution—

(1) for the reasonable cost of repeating any experimentation that was interrupted or invalidated as a result of the offense;

(2) the loss of food production or farm income reasonably attributable to the offense; and

(3) for any other economic damage resulting from the offense.

(d), (e) [Unchanged]

(As amended Oct. 11, 1996, P. L. 104-294, Title VI, § 601(r)(3), 110 Stat. 3502; June 12, 2002, P. L. 107-188, Title III, Subtitle C, § 336, 116 Stat. 681.)

HISTORY; ANCILLARY LAWS AND DIRECTIVES

Amendments:

1996. Act Oct. 11, 1996, in subsec. (c), inserted "or 3663A".

2002. Act June 12, 2002, substituted subsecs. (a) and (b) for ones which read:

"(a) Offense. Whoever—

"(1) travels in interstate or foreign commerce, or uses or causes to be used the mail or any facility in interstate or foreign commerce, for the purpose of causing physical disruption to the functioning of an animal enterprise; and

"(2) intentionally causes physical disruption to the functioning of an animal enterprise by intentionally stealing, damaging, or causing the loss of, any property (including animals or records) used by the animal enterprise, and thereby causes economic damage exceeding $10,000 to that enterprise, or conspires to do so;

shall be fined under this title or imprisoned not more than one year, or both.

"(b) Aggravated offense. (1) Serious bodily injury. Whoever in the course of a violation of subsection (a) causes serious bodily injury to another individual shall be fined under this title or imprisoned not more than 10 years, or both.

"(2) Death. Whoever in the course of a violation of subsection (a) causes the death of an individual shall be fined under this title and imprisoned for life or for any term of years.";

and, in subsec. (c), in para. (1), deleted "and" following the concluding semicolon, in para. (2), substituted "; and" for a concluding period, and added para. (3).

CODE OF FEDERAL REGULATIONS

United States Fish and Wildlife Service, Department of the Interior—Civil procedures, 50 CFR Part 11.

CROSS REFERENCES

Sentencing Guidelines for the United States Courts, 18 USCS Appx § 2B1.1.

§ 46. Transportation of water hyacinths

(a)–(c) [Unchanged]

Shall be fined under this title, or imprisoned not more than six months, or both.

(As amended Sept. 13, 1994, P. L. 103-322, Title XXXIII, § 330016(1)(G), 108 Stat. 2147.)

HISTORY; ANCILLARY LAWS AND DIRECTIVES

Amendments:

1994. Act Sept. 13, 1994, substituted "under this title" for "not more than $500".

§ 47. Use of aircraft or motor vehicles to hunt certain wild horses or burros; pollution of watering holes

(a) Whoever uses an aircraft or a motor vehicle to hunt, for the purpose of capturing or killing, any wild unbranded horse, mare, colt, or burro running at large on any of the public land or ranges shall be fined under this title, or imprisoned not more than six months, or both.

(b) Whoever pollutes or causes the pollution of any watering hole on any of the public land or ranges for the purpose of trapping, killing, wounding, or maiming any of the animals referred to in subsection (a) of this section shall be fined under this title, or imprisoned not more than six months, or both.

(c) [Unchanged]

(As amended Sept. 13, 1994, P. L. 103-322, Title XXXIII, § 330016(1)(G), 108 Stat. 2147.)

HISTORY; ANCILLARY LAWS AND DIRECTIVES

Amendments:

1994. Act Sept. 13, 1994, substituted "under this title" for "not more than $500".

CODE OF FEDERAL REGULATIONS

Bureau of Land Management, Department of the Interior—Protection, management, and control of wild free-roaming horses and burros, 43 CFR Part 4700.

Figure 3.4   Copyright 2004—Matthew Bender & Company, Inc., a member of the LexisNexis Group.

Look at Title 18, section 46 of the U.S. Code concerning "transportation of water hyacinths," reprinted in Figures 3.3 and 3.4 as it appears in the 1993 edition of the U.S.C.S. and its 2004 supplement. Note that section 46 appears in full in the main volume, but that its last sentence after subparagraph (c) also appears in the supplement. The supplement omits sections (a)–(c) noting they are "unchanged." This means that only the last sentence of the statute has been modified or amended in some way; the version of that sentence in the main volume is outdated. The version of the last sentence in the supplement is current, at least as of the date the supplement was published. Sections (a), (b), and (c) are the same in the old and new versions. Thus, to read the entire statute in its current form, you must read subsections (a), (b), and (c) in the main volume but the last sentence in the supplement.

Finding Statutes

Statutes appearing in codes are organized by subject matter. Each chapter or title begins with a table of contents. In addition, the statutes in every code are precisely indexed by name and by topic.

Many statutes have official and/or popular names. Sometimes these names relate to the statute's subject matter, as in the "Internal Revenue Code" or the "North Carolina Public Records Act." Other statutes are named after their sponsors, for example the "Sherman Antitrust Act" or the "Mann Act." You will find in most codes a **Popular Name Table** which indexes statutes by their name. Thus, if you happen to know the name of a statute, you can look it up in this index and find its location by title or chapter, and section numbers, in the code.

Often however, you will not know the name of the statute or act you are seeking. Or, you will know the name of the act, but not the location of a particular statute within that act. In such cases, the best way to find a statute is to use the **general index volumes** of the code.

Each set of statutes, no matter who publishes it, will include a set of index books. The indexes typically are located on the library shelf just after the last volume of the statute books they reference. Sometimes the indexes are not obvious; they may be a different color than the statute books, and soft-bound. When in doubt, check with the librarian.

Using the index books to find a statute seems as if it should be easy, and sometimes it is. One of the great joys in legal research is looking up the most obvious word to describe the topic you are researching and finding the statute on the first try. Other times, finding the right statute proves more difficult. The key is to develop a good list of **indexing words** to help you find all the statutes relevant to your subject matter. These words should be directly related to your subject, both specifically and generally. Try the most specific words first, and then move out to more general topics if the specific words don't work.

For example, suppose you want to know if there are any statutes requiring real estate agents to be licensed in North Carolina. What words might you look up in the index? The more you can think of, the more likely you are to find the statute, assuming of course that it exists. First try specific words like "real estate," "agent(s)," "broker(s)," or "salesperson/man." If those words fail, try something more general like "licensing," "regulation," or even "occupation." You will find a path to the statute you seek through several of these indexing words.

Practice Set 3.1

Now suppose you are looking for the statute that describes the penalties for drunk driving by a person under the age of 21. What words might you use?

_____   _____   _____

_____   _____   _____

_____   _____   _____

It is helpful to have a good vocabulary when searching an index. You might want to have a dictionary or thesaurus at hand, especially if you are having trouble finding the right word. Some indexes are better than others, and sometimes the word you would use to locate a statute isn't the one chosen by the editor of the books you are using.

If you are unable to precisely locate a statute with your indexing words, then look at the statutes that surround the ones you do find, and the **table of contents for the chapter(s)** to which the index has led you. Sometimes the statute you want is nearby. Similarly, if an index takes you to a statute that is not the right one, but seems related, take a look at the **annotations and cross-references immediately following the statute.** They may give you a clue. And, if you still cannot find a statute by using one set of books, you might try another publisher. For example, if you are using the U.S.C.A. and cannot find the statute you seek, check the index of the U.S.C.S. or U.S.C. You may have better success there.

Reading and Understanding Statutes

Once you have found the statutes you need, your next task is to read and understand them. This too can be challenging. Statutes are written not for their quality as prose, but to lay out the rules of conduct on a particular subject as thoroughly as possible. Often, the sentences are long and the structure hard to follow.

The following strategies may help you understand the meaning of a statute:

- Read slowly. Sometimes reading aloud helps.
- Find the subject and the verb of the sentence, then study the qualifying phrases or clauses. If necessary, copy the statute so that you can highlight or underline the subject and verb.

- Make note of any words like "may," "must," "unless," "if," "and," "or," "not," and "except." These words can dramatically affect the meaning of the sentence, or qualify or limit the text.

After you have read the text of the statute, refine your understanding of its meaning using the following techniques:

- Read any cross-referenced statutory sections. (Remember, they are listed in the annotations right after the statute).
- Note any conditions that must exist before the statute applies.
- Consider whether its language is mandatory ("shall," "must") or permissive ("may").
- Scan the Table of Contents to see where the statute fits within the context of its chapter and article.
- Look for a "purpose" or "policy" section for the chapter or article, to tell you why the framers of the Act felt it was important.
- Search for a "Definitions" section for information about how key words are to be read in the context of the statute.

Practice Set 3.2
(You will need access to the North Carolina General Statutes.)

Assume you have been asked to find the penalty for violation of the North Carolina Pawnbrokers statute. What should you do? Your first task is to find the statute. You might try either the general index under "pawnbroker" or the Popular Names Index under "Pawnbrokers Act." The former will take you to chapter 91A of the North Carolina General Statutes. It also reveals a "penalty" provision at § 91A-11 (chapter 91A, section 11, but referred to as "section 91A-11"). The latter will get you to Chapter 91A as well, under "Pawnbrokers Modernization Act" but will not take you directly to section 11.

Read section 11 of chapter 91A. It provides that violators of the Act are guilty of a misdemeanor and face up to a $500.00 fine, imprisonment up to six months, in the court's discretion, and in some cases, loss of pawnshop license. Do you now really understand what the statute is about? Do you know what a pawnbroker is? How does one violate the Act? When does one need a license? The answers to these questions can be found in other sections of the Act. Look at the Table of Contents for chapter 91A: there you will find that § 91A-1 gives the short title of the Act; § 91A-2 outlines its purposes; § 91A-3 provides definitions to key words used in the statute; and so on.

Exercise 3 — Finding and Reading Statutes

Locate the following statutes and constitutional provisions and answer the questions. Note any requested section numbers for North Carolina statutes in this format: § __-___, where the number before the hyphen is the chapter number, and the number following it is the section number. For example, the section number for N.C. General Statute chapter 136, section 89.48 would be written, "§ 136-89.48." (To make the "§" symbol, write an "S" and then put another "S" on top of it, so that the top of the first "S" interlocks with the bottom of the second "S.")

1. N.C. General Statues chapter 62, section 2.

   A. Section number:

   B. What does this section provide? (Summarize in one sentence. Give more than the catch-line.)

   C. When was this section originally enacted?

   D. Has this section ever been amended? If so, when was the first amendment?

   E. What is the name of the Act in which this section is contained?

   F. Give the section number in the Act that tells you the name of the Act.

2. N.C. General Statute Chapter 96, section 6.

   A. Section number:

   B. What is this section about?

   C. When was this section originally enacted?

   D. When was this section most recently amended?

   E. In what session law chapter number and section can you find the most recent amendment?

3. Use the general index to the N.C. General Statutes to locate a statute that pro-hibits a creditor from using obscene language when attempting to collect a debt. Cite the statute:

    A. Section number:

    B. What is the number of the specific subsection prohibiting obscenity?

    C. List your search terms.

4. Use the NC General Statutes' *Popular Name Index* to find the *Oil Pollution and Hazardous Substances Control Act*.

    A. Section number:

    B. What is the official title of the Act?

    C. What is the purpose of the Act?

    D. Give the section number where the "Definitions" are located.

    E. When was the Act originally enacted?

    F. Has § 143-215.79 ever been amended? If so, in what year(s)?

5. Use the general index to the N.C. General Statutes to find a statute that pro-hibits the removal of electronic dog collars.

    A. Section number (omit any lettered subsections):

    B. List your search terms.

6. Find N.C. General Statute chapter 55A, section 10-21.

    A. What is the catch-line for this statute?

    B. What type of entity does Chapter 55A address?

    C. When was section 10-21 first enacted?

7. Find Article V, section 1, of the North Carolina constitution.
   A. What is Article V about?

   B. What does section 1 prohibit, and by whom?

8. Find Title 21 of the U.S. Code Annotated, section 801.
   A. Using the Historical and Statutory Notes, find the name of the Short Title of the Act in which § 801 is contained.

   B. In what title and section are the *Definitions* for the Act?
       Title _____
       Section _____

   C. Are there any *Definitions* in the supplement (yes or no)?

   D. What is the year of the main volume and of the supplement?
       Main volume _____
       Supplement _____

9. Find the federal statute that creates the National Day of Prayer.
   A. Give the title and section numbers for the statute.
       Title _____
       Section _____

   B. What day of the year is the National Day of Prayer?

   C. When was the statute enacted?

   D. Search terms:

10. Find the Patriot Act in the *Popular Names Table*.
    A. According to the Table, what is the full name of the Patriot Act?

    B. Can the Act be found under one Title in the U.S. Code?

Chapter 4

Citing Constitutional Provisions and Statutes

(Note: Have *The Bluebook* at hand when reading this chapter.)

The Bluebook has rules of citation governing both constitutions and statutes. Constitutions are covered in Rule 11, statutes in Rule 12.

Citing Constitutional Provisions

Federal or State

Citations to constitutional provisions are relatively easy to master using *Bluebook* form. According to **Rule 11** of *The Bluebook*, if you are citing the **United States Constitution**, begin your citation with, "U.S. CONST." Remember that for practitioners, this citation is not quite right, since the main body of *The Bluebook* sets out rules for law review style citation. Unless you are working on an academic article, you must modify the rules in the main body of *The Bluebook* by looking at the *Bluepages* on the light blue pages in the front. As you will recall from Chapter 2, these rules require you to convert the typeface from large and small capital letters to ordinary roman type: "U.S. CONST." becomes "U.S. Const." Specific examples are given in B7.

If you are citing a **state constitution**, begin exactly the same way, except substitute the state's abbreviation for "U.S." The correct abbreviation for North Carolina is "N.C." as provided in table T.10 regarding geographical terms. Thus, a cite by a practitioner to the North Carolina constitution would begin, "N.C. Const." (Do not assume that every state, territory or other geographical unit is abbreviated by its postal code. Some states' abbreviations include more than two letters, e.g. "Ala." and "Mass.," and others, like Alaska and Utah, have no abbreviation at all.)

Next, give the specific part of the constitution you are citing and abbreviate it according to table T.16. This could be an article, an amendment, or an even smaller part of the constitution in question. For example, both the U.S. and North Carolina constitutions are subdivided into articles. Articles may be divided into sections, which may be further divided into clauses. In addition, both the federal and state

43

constitutions have amendments (which are sometimes divided into sections), and a preamble. Examples of citations to all these subdivisions of a constitution are provided in *The Bluebook*. For instance, the very first citation is to the 14th amendment of the United States Constitution, and is cited as, "U.S. CONST. amend. XIV, § 2."

Again, however, remember to convert the large and small capital letters into ordinary roman type in accordance with the *Bluepages*, B13: "U.S. Const." Thus, the first example in *The Bluebook* is converted by practitioners to:

U.S. Const. amend. XIV, § 2.

Likewise, the first several citations in *The Bluebook's* Rule 11 convert to:

U.S. Const. art. I, § 9, cl. 2.
U.S. Const. amend. XIV, § 2.
U.S. Const. pmbl.
N.M. Const. art. IV, § 7.[1]

As you should be able to determine by reading these examples, the first three are citations to the United States Constitution—the first to clause 2 of section 9 of article 1. The last example is to New Mexico's state constitution, article 4, section 7. Note that the citations include roman numerals for articles and amendments.

Rule 11 requires that you cite constitutional provisions currently in force without including a date. This is unusual—you will include the date of virtually every other resource you cite. For constitutional provisions, however, you need only include a date if the cited provision has been repealed or amended.

Repealed or Amended Constitutional Provisions

Repealed or amended constitutional provisions may be cited in either of the two formats demonstrated: a parenthetical stating "repealed" or "amended" and the date of repeal or amendment, or a clause set off by a comma stating, "repealed by _____" or "amended by _____" including the provision of the Constitution repealing/amending the one you are citing. *The Bluebook* examples demonstrate the rule:

U.S. Const. amend. XVIII (repealed 1933)
    or
U.S. Const. amend. XVIII, *repealed by* U.S. Const. amend. XXI

* * *

U.S. Const. art. I. § 3, cl. 1 (amended 1913)
    or
U.S. Const. art. I, § 3, cl. 1, *amended by* U.S. Const. amend. XVII, § 1.[2]

---

1. *The Bluebook: A Uniform System of Citation* R.11, at 100 (Columbia Law Review Ass'n et al. eds., 18th ed. 2005).

2. *Id.* (amended in accordance with the *Bluepages*).

In lieu of italics, it also would be perfectly correct to underscore the phrases "*repealed by*" and "*amended by,*" as in: "U.S. Const. amend. XVIII, repealed by U.S. Const. amend. XXI."

Practice Set 4.1

Cite the following Constitutional provisions:

(1) Article 2, section 11, of the North Carolina Constitution:

_____

(2) The first amendment of the United States Constitution (the one guaranteeing freedom of speech, religion, the press, etc.):

_____

(3) Article 1, section 2, clause 5 of the United States Constitution:

_____

(4) Article 14, section 1 of the North Carolina Constitution:

_____

(5) Article 1, section 19, of the North Carolina Constitution:

_____

Citing Statutes

Rule 12 of *The Bluebook* describes how to cite statutes. Because citing statutes is more complicated than citing constitutional provisions, this Rule is divided into multiple subsections. As is typical with *The Bluebook,* the first paragraph gives you examples of the correct citation form. The subsections that follow provide the details. And, section B6 of the *Bluepages* describes how practitioners should modify statutory citations.

Official and Unofficial Codes

Rules 12.1 and 12.2 of *The Bluebook* give you general guidance on what to cite. Although you can cite statutes from many sources, your first choice is either a current official or unofficial (privately published) code. **In any event, you must always cite the book you are actually using.** To cite anything other than the book you have in front of you is to misrepresent your source.

In practice, you will likely cite to an unofficial code for federal statutes (the U.S.C.A. or the U.S.C.S.), and the official code for state statutes. The official state code is the North Carolina General Statutes published by LexisNexis. The unofficial state code is published by West. It is called the *North Carolina General Statutes Annotated*. You could also cite to it, but in practice, people rarely do.

Basic Rule for Citing Statutes—Rule 12.3

The opening paragraph of **Rule 12.3** gives you the basics for citing to an official or unofficial code, and refers you to **table T.1** to find the citation format for the official and unofficial codes for each federal and state jurisdiction. According to the Rule, your citation to any statute (state or federal) must include at a minimum the:

- abbreviated name of the code as found in table T.1;
- section, paragraph, or article number(s) of the statute;
- year of the code; and
- title, chapter or volume number, if the code is so divided (see R. 12.3.1(b)).

Abbreviated Name of the Code

When citing a code, its name must be abbreviated into a universally recognizable form. For example, the United States Code becomes the "U.S.C." The *United States Code Annotated* is the "U.S.C.A." and the *United States Code Service* is the "U.S.C.S." The abbreviation for the various versions of the U.S. Code and the individual state codes (and even codes of foreign countries) are available in Table 1. Look under "Statutory Compilation" in the federal and individual state sections.

Section and Title or Chapter Numbers

Rules 12.3 and 12.3.1(b) require that you include the title or chapter or volume number if the code is so divided and also the section, paragraph, or article number of the statute. You will cite **chapter numbers** when citing **North Carolina statutes**. The chapter number is cited just before the section number, separated by a hyphen. For example, "§ 1-181" is in fact, chapter 1, section 181. Any North Carolina statutory citation should therefore always include the chapter number in front of the hyphen, and the section number following the hyphen. You will cite **title** numbers when citing federal statutes. These will appear at the very beginning of your cite, as in "15. U.S.C. § 1...." The number "15" represents the title number; "1" is the section number. Note that you will cite **section numbers in both the U.S. and North Carolina codes**—not paragraphs or articles.

Year of the Code

The last part of any statutory citation is the year of the code. This is not the date a particular statute was enacted. Rather, it is the date of the bound volume or supplement in which the statute you are citing appears. Use the year of the code appearing on the spine, if a date appears there. If not, then use the year on the title page, or if not there, the copyright year.

In practice, you may find that the year of the code is often omitted. Although *Bluebook* form demands it, check with your colleagues to determine whether you should include the year in your citations.

Citing North Carolina Statutes

The example given in Rule 12.3 of *The Bluebook* to support the basic rule of citation happens to be from North Carolina: N.C. GEN. STAT. § 1-181 (2003). Once converted to ordinary type, the example becomes:

N.C. Gen. Stat. § 1-181 (2003).

Does this citation include all the basic elements? It does:

- The abbreviated name of the code as found in table T.1: "N.C. Gen. Stat."
- The section, paragraph, or article number(s) of the statute: "181"
- The year of the code: "2003"
- The (title or) chapter number: "1"

What if no North Carolina example had been given? Information particular to North Carolina and every other state in the union, along with federal material, is available in Table 1.

Table 1

Table 1 is the largest table in *The Bluebook*. It gives detailed information on the appropriate abbreviation and format of citations to primary authorities. It begins with federal authorities, then **state** authorities for each of the fifty states, arranged alphabetically. Within each state's entry is a formula for citing that state's statutes, cases, session laws, and administrative materials. In the 18th edition of *The Bluebook*, the North Carolina section begins on page 224.

Each state's entry begins with its courts, followed by its statutes. Turn to the North Carolina entry in T.1 and look for North Carolina's statutory compilation to find the abbreviation for the North Carolina General Statutes. As you will note, the first example in Table 1 matches the example in the main body of Rule 12.3. This is to the official North Carolina statutes. The Table indicates that the correct abbreviation and format for the citation (converted to comport with the *Bluepages*) is:

N.C. Gen. Stat. § x-x (year).

The second example is to the unofficial West publication of the statutes. Again, the convention in this state is to cite the chapter and section number together, with a hyphen separating the two, immediately after the "§" symbol. Thus, the "x-x" in both examples includes first the chapter number, then the section number, separated by a hyphen, as in "§ 1-181." Remember, this is really chapter 1, section 181 but is shortened to "§ 1-181" in common parlance and in the citation.

Some sections are themselves divided by a hyphen. For example, if you see a citation that looks like this: "N.C. Gen. Stat. § 55A-10-21 (2004)," that means that the statute can be found in chapter 55A, section 10-21. The first number following the "§" symbol will always be the chapter number. Any numbers after the first hyphen are section numbers.

Practice Set 4.2

Look at the following two North Carolina citations, and name the chapter and section number for each one:

(1) N.C. Gen. Stat. § 93A-6(a) (2003)

       chapter: _____; section: _____

(2) N.C. Gen. Stat. § 25-2-101 (2003)

       chapter: _____; section: _____

Practice Set 4.3

Cite section 14-11 of the North Carolina General Statutes on the line below, assuming it appears in the 2003 volume of the statute book:

_____

Practice Set 4.4

Assume that you are asked to cite section 610.320 of the Kentucky statutes, and that it comes from the 2004 volume. What will your citation look like? Look up South Carolina in Table T.1, and go to its "Statutory Compilation." Look at the model, and then write your answer here.

_____

What if you have to cite a statute from another state? Go to Table 1, and look up the "statutory compilation" for the state in question. There you will see the proper abbreviation and format for that state's statutes.

Publisher

When citing the Kentucky statute, why did you have to include "West" in the parenthetical with the date? Because while North Carolina has an **official** code (N.C. Gen. Stat.), Kentucky does not. The *Baldwin's Kentucky Revised Statutes Annotated* is an **unofficial** publication. Because it is unofficial, *Bluebook* rules require that you note the publisher in the parentheses, just like the U.S.C.S.[3]

---

3. *Id.* R. 12.3.1(d), at 105.

Citing Federal Statutes

To find the rules for citing federal statutes, go back to the basic rule—Rule 12.3. Remember that regardless of whether you are citing a state or federal statute, you must include the name of the code as per Table T.1, the section, paragraph or article number of the statute, the year of the code, and the title, chapter or volume number. In this case, the rule specifies that you cite the title of the U.S. Code **before** the name of the code and gives the following examples:

> 42 U.S.C. § 1983 (2000)
> 12 U.S.C.S. § 1719 (LexisNexis 1993 & Supp. 2004).[4]

For further detail on citing federal statutes, you can return to Table T.1. You will find the **federal section** at the beginning of the table. The entry for federal statutory compilations tells you to cite to the U.S. Code "if therein," reinforcing *The Bluebook's* preference that you cite statutes to a code rather than session laws. Each of the major codes is listed on the left, with a sample of how to cite it on the right, including the abbreviated name of the code. The 'x' is used to designate where numbers should go.

The following are the examples as they appear in Table 1 of *The Bluebook:*

> x U.S.C. § x (year)
> x U.S.C.A. § x (West year)
> x U.S.C.S. § x (Law. Co-op. year)
> x U.S.C.U. § x (Gould year).[5]

The first "x" in each of the examples is for the title number in question. Since there are fifty titles, that number will always be a number from 1 to 50. The symbol "§" stands for "section." The parentheses at the end always include the **date of the code** (not the date the statute was enacted). Unless the code is the official one, you must also identify the **publisher** of the code inside the parentheses in the manner shown, along with the date of the code. Thus, a cite to the U.S.C.A. will always include the word "West" as the first thing inside the parentheses. A cite to the U.S.C.S. will always include "LexisNexis."

---

4. *Id.* R. 12.3.1(b), at 104.
5. *Id.* T.1, at 196.

Practice Set 4.5

Practice with the following citation to Title 15, section 1001 of the U.S. Code. For practice sake, assume that it appears entirely within the 1994 main volume of the official U.S. Code (not the supplement), and the 1997 main volumes of the U.S.C.A. and U.S.C.S. How would you cite this title and section from (1) the U.S. Code, (2) the U.S. Code Annotated, and (3) the U.S. Code Service? Write your answers below:

(1) _____

(2) _____

(3) _____

Citing Statutes in Supplements

When citing a statute, you usually cite it as it is currently in force. Often, all or part of the most current version of statute will be in the supplement rather than the main volume. In any event, cite to the place or places your reader must look in order to find the current statute.

Bluebook **Rule 12.3.1(e)** directs you to cite materials in supplements according to **Rule 3.1(c)**. This cross-reference from Rule 12 to Rule 3 illustrates an annoying but important feature of *The Bluebook*: general rules of citation that apply universally to all legal authorities are contained in Rules 1–9. Those that are specific to a particular type of authority follow. In this case, Rule 12 deals particularly with statutes, while Rule 3 deals generally with "subdivisions," including supplements, whether for statutes, books, or other resources.

Rule 3.1(c) requires that when you cite to material appearing in a supplement (or pocket part), you must put the abbreviation "Supp." inside the date parenthetical, along with the date of the supplement.

Look at the example given for the Hawaii Revised Statutes (converted here to ordinary roman type): "Haw. Rev. Stat. § 296-46.1 (Supp. 1984)." The fact that "Supp. 1984" appears inside the parenthetical means that this particular citation refers to chapter 296, section 46.1 of a Hawaii statute as it appeared in its entirety in a 1984 supplement. Obviously, this is not a cite to a current supplement. Nevertheless, it provides an example of the correct format for a citation to a statute that appears in full in a supplement to the main volume.

Because the North Carolina statute books publish revised statutes in their entirety in the supplement, citations to North Carolina General Statutes will nearly always follow one of the following two formats:

(1) For statutes where no changes have been made and nothing is in the supplement other than notes and/or annotations: N.C. Gen. Stat. § 14-27.1 (2003);

(2) For statutes where some part of the statute has been changed, and the entire statute is reprinted in the supplement: N.C. Gen. Stat. § 14-27.2 (Supp. 2004).

(Remember that the official North Carolina statute books are currently reprinted every other year. Thus, for the odd numbered years, there will be no supplement, as the statute books are all brand new. In the even numbered years, there will be a supplement. The hardbound edition is likely to have its supplement in a pocket part, while the softbound edition will have its supplement in a separate two-volume set.)

What about federal statutes? If a federal statute has not been amended from the time the book in which it appears was published, follow the basic citation format:

15 U.S.C. § 1 (1994)

If the statute is reprinted in its entirety in the supplement (an unlikely scenario unless the statute is very short or the whole thing has been changed) cite only the supplement in the parenthetical. The following are representative examples:

15 U.S.C.A. § 7214 (West Supp. 2004)

18 U.S.C.S. § 37 (LexisNexis Supp. 2004).

And, if you need to cite a federal statute that has been recently amended, such that part of the statute (but not all) appears in the supplement, cite both the main volume **and** the supplement. This tells your reader to look in both places to find the statute as it currently exists:

11 U.S.C.A. § 503 (West 1993 & Supp. 2004).

To read this statute in its entirety as it is currently in force, you must read the amended sections in the supplement, and the sections that have not been amended (from the time the main volume was published) in the main volume.

Citing Multiple Sections and Subsections — *Bluebook* Rule 3.3(b)

Often, the answer to a particular statutory question will be found in more than one section. Sometimes these sections will be side by side, or at least within the same chapter and article. Other times, they may be widely separated throughout the code. *The Bluebook* gives guidance on citing multiple sections and subsections in Rule 3.3(b).

Suppose that you are asked to find the statutes governing the conduct of veterinarians. By looking up the word "veterinarian" in the index to the NC General Statutes, you will be directed to various provisions in Chapter 90. Specifically, you will find that the North Carolina Veterinary Practice Act occupies sections 179 through 187.15. Using *Bluebook* Rule 3.3(b), how do you cite the whole Act? Look at *The Bluebook* rule reprinted in the box below.[6]

---

6. *Id.* R. 3.3(b), at 62. (Citation type-style changed to ordinary roman type in accordance with the *Bluepages.*)

Rule 3.3(b) — Multiple Sections and Subsections

When citing consecutive sections or subsections, use two section symbols (§§). Give inclusive numbers; do not use "*et seq.*" Identical digits or letters preceding a punctuation mark may be omitted, unless doing so would create confusion. Otherwise, retain all digits.

> Wash. Rev. Code Ann. §§ 18.51.005–.52.900 (West 1989 & Supp. 1991).

> Del. Code Ann. tit. 9, §§ 817–819 (1989).

Note that letters are sometimes used to designate sections, rather than subsections, and that section designations may contain punctuation within them:

> 42 U.S.C. §§ 1396a–1396d (1994).

If an en dash or hyphen would be ambiguous, use the word "to":

> 42 U.S.C. §§ 1973aa-2 to -4 (1994)

> Mont. Code Ann. §§ 75-1-301 to -324 (1989).

When citing scattered sections, separate the sections with commas:

> N.J. Stat. Ann. §§ 18A:54-1, -3, -6 (West 1989).

Repeat digits if necessary to avoid confusion:

> N.J. Stat. Ann. §§ 18A:58-17, :58-25, :64A-22.1, :64A-22.6 (West 1989).

Examine the first citation in the box — it is a citation to the Washington statutory compilation (the Washington Revised Code Annotated). The statute cited begins at section 18.51.005 and ends at section 18.52.900. In order to convey this to the reader, the citation includes two section symbols ("§§") to indicate that more than section is cited, and omits the number "18" from the second half of the citation in accordance with the provision allowing omission of identical numbers preceding a punctuation mark. Hence, the idea of "section 18.51.005 through section 18.51.900" is conveyed as "§§ 18.51.005–.51.900."

Practice Set 4.6

Apply *Bluebook* Rule 3.3(b) to the citation of the North Carolina Veterinary Practice Act (codified at sections 90-179 through 90-187.15) and write your citation to the whole Act below, assuming that the entire Act appears in the 2003 main volume and that there are no changes in the supplement. Note that the sections of the Washington statute contain no hyphens while North Carolina's statutes do. How can you make your citation to the North Carolina Act clear?

If you cited the North Carolina Veterinary Practice Act as N.C. Gen. Stat. §§ 90-179–187.15 (2003) you have made an error. If you don't add the word "to" between the section numbers, a person who read your citation could assume that you were citing only one section. In fact, individual North Carolina statutes often contain two hyphens. For example, a citation to any **one** section in the Business Corporation Act always contains two hyphens, e.g. N.C. Gen. Stat. § 55-1-1 (2003). This citation is to chapter 55, section 1-1, of the Act. Thus, a person reading the citation, "§§ 90-179–187.15" might think you were citing chapter 90, section 179-187.5, despite the two "§" symbols. Instead, follow the portion of the rule in 3.4(b) exemplified by the Montana example, and cite the North Carolina Veterinary Practice Act as: N.C. Gen. Stat. §§ 90-179 to -187.15 (2003).

In your citation of the Veterinary Practice Act, you can omit the "90" in front of -187.15 because you've already given it once and it comes before the hyphen. (The rule says, " Identical digits or letters preceding a punctuation mark may be omitted, unless doing so would create confusion."[7]) However, don't break up a single number in the middle. For example, if you are citing sections 180 through 185, you may not say, "§§ 90-180 to -85" (omitting the "1" in front of "85.") Even though you might speak this way, the citation is not sufficiently clear. This is expressly prohibited by *The Bluebook* in the Delaware example. Instead, write it as, "§§ 90-180 to -185."

When citing sections scattered within a single chapter, separate each one with a comma. Again, you may omit identical numbers or letters preceding a punctuation mark.

Practice Set 4.7

Try citing sections 182, 185 and 187 of the Veterinary Practice Act here:

When citing **sections scattered among several chapters or titles**, you will need to repeat digits preceding a punctuation mark to avoid confusion. For example, N.C. Gen. Stat. §§ 90-185, 89C-1, 93A-4 (2003).

When citing multiple subsections within one section, use only one section symbol. Thus, N.C. Gen. Stat. § 90-185(1), (2), (4), (6) (2003) is the correct citation form, because all these subsections are part of one section, i.e. section 185. But, if citing multiple subsections within different sections, then use two section symbols. Thus, N.C. Gen. Stat. §§ 90-185(2), -186(3) (2004), is correct.

---

7. *Id.*

Name of the Act

On occasion, the name of the statute may be required as part of your statutory citation, but:

> ...only if the statute is commonly cited that way or the information would otherwise aid in identification. Omit "The" as the first word of a statute's name. An official name, a popular name, or both may be used:
>
>> Labor Management Relations (Taft-Hartley) Act § 301(a), 29 U.S.C. § 185(a) (1988)
>>
>> Occupational Safety and Health Act (OSHA) of 1970, 29 U.S.C. § 651 (2000).[8]

In general, omit the name of the statute.

Special Citation Forms — Rule 12.8

The Internal Revenue Code

Title 26 of the U.S. Code is the Internal Revenue Code. *The Bluebook's* Rule 12.8.1 allows an alternative form to the traditional citation: namely, "I.R.C." followed by the section number and year. Thus, both of the following options are a correct citation of Title 26, section 401(k):

- 26 U.S.C. § 401(k) (2000)
- I.R.C. § 401(k) (2000).

If you are using an unofficial reporter such as the U.S.C.A. or U.S.C.S., you must so note in the date parenthetical:

- 26 U.S.C.A. § 401(k) (West Supp. 2004)
- I.R.C. § 401(k) (West Supp. 2004).

In this case, because section 401(k) is reprinted with changes in the supplement, "Supp." appears in the parentheses along with "West" and the date, in the order shown above.

Federal and State Procedural Rules

The laws of both the state and federal governments include procedural rules governing the conduct of a case through the courts. These include rules governing the procedure to follow when pursuing a civil or criminal case, the type of evidence that can be used during a trial, and the rules governing the appeal process. Although some of these rules are created legislatively, and others are created in the judicial system, they all can be cited in the same basic format, in accordance with Rule 12.8.3. Remember to convert to ordinary type. Thus, the following examples are correct for practitioners for the rules of civil, criminal and appellate procedure, and the rules of evidence:

---

8. *Id.* R. 12.3.1, at 104.

- Fed. R. Civ. P. 12(b)(6)
- N.C. R. Civ. P. 12(b)(6)

- Fed. R. Crim. P. 42(a)
- N.C. R. Crim P. 42(a)

- Fed. R. App. P. 2
- N.C. R. App. P. 2

- Fed. R. Evid. 410
- N.C. R. Evid. 410

The citation of state and federal rules is exactly the same except that in the case of state rules, "N.C." replaces "Fed." No date is required.

Citation of Session Laws — Rule 12.4

Session laws are the body of laws enacted by a state or federal legislature during its annual or biennial legislative session. These are published separately at the end of each session, before the laws are codified into subject matter codes.

The North Carolina session laws organize all the acts of the North Carolina General Assembly from a particular session in chronological order according to the date passed. The federal session laws, known as the "Statutes at Large" are likewise published separately and in chronological order.

Occasionally, it may be necessary to cite either state or federal session laws. Cite to the North Carolina Session Laws or the Federal Statutes at Large when (1) you have to cite to a newly enacted law or amendment not yet codified into the General Statutes or United States Code; or (2) you have to cite a previous version of the law that is no longer in effect. Otherwise, cite to the subject matter code, namely the United States Code or the North Carolina General Statutes.

Citing the Federal Statutes at Large

Rule 12.4(a) of *The Bluebook* requires that when you cite a session law, you **always** "give the name of the statute and the public law or chapter number.... An official name, a popular name, or both may be used."[9] This is different from citing statutes. You must include the name of the law in any session law cite; you don't typically have to do so when citing a codified statute.

The name of the Act can be hard to find. Look for it in the body of the Act itself, especially in the early sections, or, in the notes following the Act. If you cannot find an official name or a popular name, identify the statute by its date of enactment, e.g. "Act of August 21, 1974."

Your cite for a session law will include either a public law number or chapter number, depending upon the year of the session law. Before 1957, federal statutes at

---

9. *Id.* R. 12.4(a), at 106.

large were laid out in chapters. The correct formula for citing pre-1957 federal session laws is:

> Name of the Act, ch. x, y Stat. z (year).

In this example, x is the chapter number, y is the volume of the Statutes at Large in which the session law appears, "Stat." is the abbreviation for "Statutes at Large," and z is the page number on which the session law appears. Unlike codified statutes, the date is the date of enactment, not the date of book. The final product, as exemplified in *The Bluebook*, looks like this:

> White-Slave Traffic (Mann) Act, ch. 395, 36 Stat. 825 (1910) (codified as amended at 18 U.S.C. §§ 2421–2424 (1994)).[10]

When citing a **particular section or subsection** of a session, add the section number to your cite after the chapter or public law number, and add the page number on which it appears if not the same page as the beginning of the Act:

> Sherman Act, ch. 647, § 1, 26 Stat. 209 (1890).
> Sherman Act, ch. 647, § 7, 26 Stat. 209, 210 (1890).[11]

Beginning in 1957, public law numbers replaced chapter numbers. Otherwise, the formula is the same:

> Name of the Act, Pub. L. No. xx-xxx, y Stat. z (year).

The public law number, as illustrated by "xx-xxxx," is always hyphenated. The number in front of the hyphen is the number of the Congress that passed the Act. The number immediately following the hyphen is the chronological number of the Act. For example, Pub. L. No. 91-190 is the 190th law passed by the 91st Congress. As before, "y" is the volume of the Statutes at Large in which the session law appears, and "z" is the page number. Here are the examples from Rule 12.4(b) in *The Bluebook* citing first the whole of Public Law Number 91-190, and then citing just section 102 of that law:

> National Environmental Policy Act of 1969, Pub. L. No. 91-190, 83 Stat. 852 (1970).

> National Environmental Policy Act of 1969, Pub. L. No. 91-190, § 102, 83 Stat. 852, 853–54 (1970).[12]

(Although *The Bluebook* forbids omission of the first digit in a multi-digit number when citing a statutory section, it permits it for the page numbers here. Thus you may say, "853–54" rather than "853–854.")

Citing State Session Laws

Citation of state session laws follows a formula similar to that for federal Statutes at Large. As set forth in table T.1 in the North Carolina section of *The Bluebook*, the correct abbreviation is, "N.C. Sess. Laws." The same difficulty exists with North

---

10. *Id.*
11. See *id.* R. 12.4(b), at 107.
12. *Id.*

Carolina session laws as with federal Statutes at Large: they were numbered as chapters until 1998, and thereafter numbered as public law numbers. Because the volume number of the session law is the year it was enacted, no date is needed at the end of the citation; it would be duplicative.

Format: Name, ch. x, year N.C. Sess. Laws page no.

Here are two examples, the first a recent statute numbered as a "public law," and the second, an older statute numbered as a "chapter:"

Uniform Electronic Transactions Act, Pub. L. No. 2003-233, 2003 N.C. Sess. Laws 400.

Public Hospital Personnel Act, ch. 517, 1997 N.C. Sess. Laws 2290.

If you are citing a particular section within a North Carolina session law, add it in the same place you would in a federal statute at large—after the public law or chapter number—segregated by commas. Give both the page number on which the session law begins, and if different, the page number(s) on which the cited section appears:

Uniform Electronic Transactions Act, Pub. L. No. 2003-233, § 1, 2003 N.C. Sess. Laws 400.

Public Hospital Personnel Act, ch. 517, § 2, 1997 N.C. Sess. Laws 2290, 2290–2293.

Exercise 4 — Citing Statutes

Using the official North Carolina General Statutes and the unofficial *United States Code Annotated*, locate the following statutes and constitutional provisions. For each one, cite the section or provision in *Bluebook* form and answer the other questions.

1. Find the NC statute that dictates the number of members on the state licensing board for veterinarians.

    A. Citation:

    B. When was this section originally enacted?

    C. Has this section ever been amended? If so, when was the most recent amendment?

    D. How many members are on the board? Who appoints them?

    E. What search terms did you use to find the statute?

2. Find the NC statutes that requires manufacturers of toxic household cleaners to put a "caution" label on their products.

    A. Citation:

    B. What is the penalty for violating the statute? (Answer the question and cite the section of the statute that lays out the penalty.)

    C. List your search terms.

3. Find the specific subsection of an NC statute that requires landlords to put operable smoke detectors in residential rental properties.

    A. Citation:

    B. Search terms:

4. In North Carolina, which state officials can be impeached?

    A. Answer the question here.

B. Cite the statute that answers the question.

C. Search terms:

5. Find the North Carolina Wage and Hour Act.
    A. Citation:

    B. Search terms:

6. Find the NC statute that requires a personal representative under a will to per-
    form his or her duties in a reasonable and prudent manner.
    A. Citation:

    B. Search terms:

8. Find the federal statute that protects the graves of Native Americans.
    A. Cite the whole Act, including all sections:

    B. What is the name of the Act?

    C. Search terms:

9. Find Title 18 of the U.S. Code Annotated, section 115
    A. Citation:

    B. Cite subsection 115(a):

    C. Cite subsection 115(b):

    D. Cite subsection 115(c):

10. Find Title 12 of the U.S. Code Annotated or U.S. Code Service, section 1831a.
    A. Cite subsection (a) of section 1831a.

    B. Cite subsection (c)(3)(B).

C.   What does subsection (c)(3)(B) say? (Quote the words of the subsection.)

11. Find the United States Constitution.
    A. Cite the Sixth Amendment.

    B. What does it provide?

Chapter 5

Cases: Reporters and Digests

Have you ever had to go to court? Perhaps you got a speeding ticket, appeared as a witness, or even sued somebody. Whether you were in criminal court over a ticket, or civil court as part of a lawsuit, the action in which you were involved was a "case."

According to *Black's Law Dictionary* 195 (5th ed. 1979), the term "case" means *inter alia* (among other things):

- a general term for an action, cause, suit or controversy at law or equity...;
- a question contested before a court of justice....;
- a judicial proceeding for the determination of a controversy between parties wherein rights are enforced or protected, or wrongs are prevented or redressed;
- any proceeding judicial in its nature.

Cases are generally classified as "civil" or "criminal." A third category of cases, "administrative," is addressed later in this book. **Civil cases** are those brought by one or more private citizens (the "plaintiff(s)") against other citizens (the "defendant(s)") seeking some sort of remedy or redress for a perceived wrong. The remedies sought in civil cases may be monetary damages, or injunctive relief (i.e., to make the defendant stop doing something). **Criminal cases** are brought by the state or federal government for violation of a penal law by an alleged wrongdoer (the "defendant"). The remedies sought include fines payable to the government, and/or imprisonment.

Every year, millions of civil and criminal cases are instituted across the country. Some are handled in a matter of weeks, but most take months or years to resolve. Those not settled are ultimately tried before a trial court, which renders a written decision. It typically includes *Findings of Fact*, *Conclusions of Law*, and an *Order*.

A significant number of tried cases are appealed by the loser. Most of these appeals are heard by an intermediate appellate court, which renders its own written decision, called an "opinion." Opinions of intermediate appellate courts can be appealed to a higher appellate court, which also renders a written opinion. The written decisions of some trial courts, and virtually all appellate courts, are published in books called *reporters*. These books are readily available for study and their contents make up the body of law known as "case law."

North Carolina Trial Courts

The North Carolina court system consists of two divisions: the trial division and the appellate division. Within the trial division are three levels of courts: small claims, district and superior. The appellate division includes two courts: the North Carolina Court of Appeals (an intermediate appellate court), and the Supreme Court (the highest North Carolina court).

In the trial division, Small Claims Courts (also known as Magistrates Courts) hear civil cases where the amount in controversy is $5000.00 or less. Many litigants appear without lawyers. The subject matter is limited to complaints for money owed, actions to recover specific personal property, and actions to evict residential tenants from rental property ("summary ejectment"). Cases are heard by a magistrate rather than a jury, and if either party is unhappy with the outcome, he or she can appeal to district court, where the trial will be heard all over again (trial *de novo*). Magistrates can also hear minor criminal matters: they accept guilty pleas for low-level misdemeanors and traffic violations, and accept waivers of trial for "worthless check" cases.

District Courts hear civil, criminal and juvenile cases. Civil cases are limited to those where the amount in controversy is less than $10,000.00, including domestic law cases involving divorce, child support and custody. Civil jury trials are available in Civil District Court. Criminal District Court cases involve infractions or misdemeanors, and no jury trial is available.

Superior Courts hear civil cases where the amount in controversy is $10,000.00 or more. They also hear all felony criminal cases, and appeals of criminal infractions and misdemeanors. Juries are allowed in both civil and criminal cases, although they are often waived in civil cases.

All three trial courts render written decisions. However, in North Carolina, these decisions are not collected and published in a form accessible to most researchers. Rather, they must be obtained on a case-by-case basis from the deciding court.

North Carolina Appellate Courts

Appeals from the District and Superior Courts are to the North Carolina Court of Appeals. (Exceptions include capital murder cases in Superior Court where appeal of the death penalty is straight to the North Carolina Supreme Court, and certain District Court cases which are first appealed to Superior Court for a new trial.) The Court of Appeals is made up of fifteen judges who hear appeals in panels of three. The Court of Appeals does not hear the testimony of witnesses or receive evidence, as a trial court does. Rather, it reviews the trial transcript and evidence submitted at trial and hears the arguments of each side to determine whether the trial judge made an error applying the law. According to the North Carolina Administrative Office of the Courts, in fiscal year 2003–2004, the Court of Appeals received more than seventeen hundred fifty appeals.

Litigants who are unhappy with the Court of Appeals' decision can ask the North Carolina Supreme Court to hear their appeal. The North Carolina Supreme Court has seven justices—a chief justice and six associate justices. It is the state's highest court. There is no further appeal in the state from its decisions. It hears appeals of North Carolina constitutional questions, and cases where the three judges on the Court of Appeals panel did not all agree with the result. The Supreme Court has discretion to hear other appeals and decides whether to take them based on whether there is a significant public interest or legal question at stake, and, whether the Court of Appeals' decision conflicts with a decision of the Supreme Court.

A chart outlining the North Carolina courts and routes of appeal is available on the Web at:

http://www.nccourts.org/Courts/Appellate/Supreme/Routes.asp.

North Carolina Appellate Court Opinions

Like other appellate courts, the North Carolina appellate courts issue written decisions which are gathered together and published in reporters. These books are readily accessible to researchers. Of course, it takes time for a decision to be published into a hardbound volume. Before each opinion appears in the hardbound reporter, it is available from other sources.

Initially, appellate court opinions can be obtained from the courts themselves. Opinions of the appellate courts are issued more or less chronologically on "slips" of ordinary 8½ x 11 inch paper, known as "slip opinions" or "slip decisions." They are available from the issuing court as soon as the written opinion is rendered. Too, the North Carolina appellate courts now publish their written decisions on the internet at:

http://www.aoc.state.nc.us/www/public/html/opinions.htm.

Court of Appeals cases are available on the Web from 1996 forward, Supreme Court cases from 1997 forward. You do not have to be a subscriber to a special service or have LEXIS or Westlaw to get them. All you need is a computer with web access.

Over time, the printed slip opinions are gathered together and printed in soft-bound pamphlets call **Advance Sheets**. Advance sheets are printed every week or so in "advance" of the hard bound volume of the official and unofficial reporters, and are issued to libraries and other reporter subscribers. They contain the full text of 20–30 opinions, and often include many other decisions published without a written opinion. Each case looks exactly as it will ultimately appear in the hardbound reporter, including the same text, typeface and page numbers.

When enough cases are issued to fill three or four advance sheets, these are compiled into a hardbound volume. That volume will be given the next chronological volume number in the series.

North Carolina Official and Unofficial Reporters

North Carolina cases appear in two different reporters: the official reporters published on behalf of the state, and the unofficial reporters published by West. The official and unofficial reporters are organized differently.

Official Reporters — "N.C. App." and "N.C."

The official reporters are divided into two sets, the *North Carolina Court of Appeals Reports* ("N.C. App.") containing only Court of Appeals opinions, and a separate *North Carolina Reports* ("N.C.") containing only North Carolina Supreme Court opinions.

The cover of the North Carolina Court of Appeals reporter ("N.C. App.") is always green, as is the cover of the companion advance sheets. The North Carolina Supreme Court reporter ("N.C.") is tan, but inexplicably, its companion advance sheets come in a light blue cover. The advance sheets are three-hole-punched and are typically found in black, loose-leaf binders, after the most recently published hardbound reporter on the shelf.

Unofficial Reporters

The North Carolina cases also are published privately by West Publishing Company in an unofficial reporter called the *South Eastern Reporter*. This reporter is published in an original ("S.E.") and a second series ("S.E.2d"). Advance sheets for the *South Eastern Reporter* are published approximately once each week.

The South Eastern Reporter is one of seven regional reporters published by West covering State court opinions from each of the fifty states: the Atlantic (A.), North Eastern (N.E.), North Western (N.W.), Pacific (P.), Southern (So.), South Western (S.W.) and South Eastern (S.E.). The *South Eastern Reporter* includes state appellate court decisions from North Carolina, South Carolina, Georgia, Virginia, and West Virginia.

The *South Eastern Reporter* includes both North Carolina Court of Appeals and Supreme Court cases from each of the five states. The original series consists of 200 volumes, including cases up to early 1939. The second series contains more recent cases. It is generally referred to as the "South East Second," and currently includes more than 600 volumes.

A limited *North Carolina Reporter,* and *North Carolina Reporter 2d*, published by West, is also available containing the opinions exactly as they appear in the *South Eastern Reporter*, but including only North Carolina opinions and omitting those from the other four states in the region. The pagination is the same in both West reporters. Thus, in the North Carolina version, there will be gaps in page numbers where the cases from other states would appear in the South Eastern version.

Federal Courts

The federal courts are organized much like the North Carolina courts. Federal trial courts are known as "District Courts." Each state in the country has at least one federal district court. More populous states have more districts. North Carolina has three federal district courts: the Eastern, Middle and Western Districts of North Carolina ("E.D.N.C.," "M.D.N.C." and "W.D.N.C.," respectively). Federal district courts hear cases involving a federal question and cases where the litigants have "diversity of citizenship" (i.e., they are from more than one state or country) and the amount in controversy between them exceeds $75,000.00.

Appeals from each district court go to a particular U.S. Court of Appeals, depending primarily on geography. For example, all District Court cases tried in any of the three districts in North Carolina (Eastern, Middle or Western) go to the United States Court of Appeals for the Fourth Circuit. The Fourth Circuit also hears cases from each of the federal district courts in West Virginia, Virginia, Maryland, and South Carolina. There are thirteen federal circuits. Numbers one through eleven hear cases from the federal courts in groups of neighboring states, like the Fourth Circuit. There is also a D.C. Circuit for cases in the District of Columbia, and a Federal Circuit which hears specific types of cases from all the federal judicial districts.

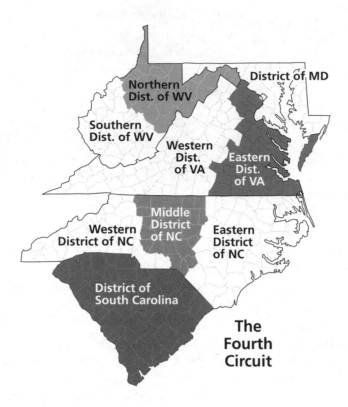

Federal Court Opinions

Unlike North Carolina state court opinions, federal court opinions are available for the District (trial) courts, as well as the U.S. Courts of Appeal and Supreme Court. There is greater demand for these opinions, and perhaps a belief that overall, they are more important.

Federal cases are reported in various reporters, most of which are published by West. **District Court** cases of general interest are published in West's *Federal Supplement*. The *Federal Supplement* includes both an original series up to volume 999 ("F. Supp."), and a second series ("F. Supp. 2d"). **U.S. Court of Appeals** cases of interest are published in West's *Federal Reporter*. The *Federal Reporter* includes the original 300 volume series containing the oldest cases ("F."), a 999-volume second series containing cases from 1924 to 1993 ("F.2d"), and a third series containing the most recent cases ("F.3d.").

The **United States Supreme Court** opinions are published in three separate reporters: the official *United States Reports* ("U.S."); West's unofficial *Supreme Court Reporter* ("S. Ct."); and the LexisNexis® Group's *United States Supreme Court Reports, Lawyers Edition* ("L. Ed.") (copyright Matthew Bender & Co.) which also has a second series for more recent cases ("L. Ed. 2d"). Opinions in the unofficial reporters have references in their text indicating the page number you would be on were you reading the case from the official reporter. This enables you to more easily cite cases in the official reporter, even if you are reading them in an unofficial one.

In addition to the reporters described above, there are a number of specialized federal reporters. These include the:

- *Federal Rules Decisions* ("F.R.D.") containing opinions about the federal rules of procedure;
- *Military Justice Reporter* ("M.J.") containing opinions of the U.S. Court of Military Appeals and other military courts;
- *Bankruptcy Reporter* ("Bankr.") containing opinions of the U.S. Bankruptcy Court;
- *Court of International Trade Reports* ("Ct. Int'l Trade") and prior iterations; and
- *U.S. Claims Court Reporter* containing cases of claims made against the United States.

Organization of a Reporter

Pick up any reporter, either official or unofficial, and you will see a number of consistent features. On the spine you will find the volume number. Inside, near the front, you will find a table of the cases reported within the volume, listed alphabetically, a table listing each of the statutes construed by the court in the opinions within the volume, and a table of the court rules considered by the court in any of those cases. At the back of the book, after the reported opinions, you will find two indexes to the cases within the volume: an analytical index consisting of summaries of the important points of each case, and a "words and phrases" index for locating cases based upon their subject matter.

The indexes inside a particular volume of any reporter are useful only to a limited extent. There are hundreds of reporters covering North Carolina appellate opinions, and hundreds more covering federal opinions. If you know that the case you want is in a particular volume but you don't know on what page, the indexes will help you. But if you need an opinion on a particular topic, and you don't know in which book to look, it is impractical to search the index of each book until you find all the cases on your topic. For such a search, you need a "digest." Digests are addressed below.

Organization of a Reported Case

Each reported case begins with a caption setting out the names of each of the plaintiffs, and each of the defendants, and any other parties to the matter. Next is a docket number: an internal indexing number used by the courts. The docket number also is used by the parties to the case and may be helpful to researchers seeking detailed information about it directly from the court. Immediately following the docket number is the date the opinion was filed. Next are short summaries of the important points of the case known as "headnotes," a summary of the origin of the appeal, the names of the attorneys for the parties, the name of the judge or justice who authored the court's opinion, and finally, the actual opinion. Look for each of these features in Figure 5.1 (the beginning of a North Carolina Supreme Court opinion published by LexisNexis in the official North Carolina Reports), and Figure 5.2 (the beginning of the same case in the unofficial West South Eastern Reporter).

Although the text of the opinion in the official and unofficial reporter will be identical, the opinions are organized differently. For instance, the same opinion will appear in a different volume number of the two reporters, and on different page numbers. In addition, the information appearing before the text of the actual court opinion will not be the same across the two reporters.

Headnotes

In both reporters, at the beginning of each reported case before the actual opinion, you will find numbered summaries of the key issues and points of law covered by the court. These are called "**headnotes**." The summaries are created by the respective editors of the reporters, and are often quite different from one another in number and in substance for the same reported decision. Each headnote is numbered in order of its appearance at the beginning of the case, and also carries a separate subject matter topic and number.

Both the official and unofficial reporters use a comprehensive numbering system for headnotes. West calls its system "**key numbers**." Each headnote in a West reporter (e.g., the *South Eastern Reporter*) has a bold-letter topic, followed by a key-shaped icon and a number. These topics and numbers correspond with the subject matter covered in the cases. West categorizes cases into more than 400 major topics. Each topic is subdivided into a multitude of sub-topics. As a result, there are thousands of key numbers, each concerning a precise point of law.

For example, a case concerning whether an automobile racetrack is a "nuisance" will be classified under the topic "nuisance," key number 3(9). All cases from every court in the country concerning the question of whether an automobile racetrack is a nuisance bear the same key number and topic if they are published by West. Similarly, cases concerning the prosecution's right to raise objections after sentencing will be classified under "criminal law," key number 996(3). Cases involving removal of an executor or administrator of an estate will be found under "Executors and Administrators," key number 35(15). Any topic that has been reported will be classified and numbered according to the West key numbering system. The West key numbers can be used to find other cases and resources on the same or similar topics. (See the discussion of Digests below, and Chpt. 9.)

Likewise, the headnote numbers in the official reporters can be cross-referenced to other resources published by the same publishing company. Most significant is a series called *Strong's North Carolina Index* which serves as a mechanism for finding cases. It is discussed at length below.

JONES *v.* SPEEDWAYS, INC.

MURLE B. JONES, MARY H. JONES, GEORGE W. JONES, EDRIE B. JONES, THOMAS G. GINN, VIRGINIA P. GINN, MR. & MRS. ROGER D. GINN, W. JACK WINGATE, PEARL D. WINGATE, L. P. WOFFORD, GWENDOLYN B. WOFFORD, MR. & MRS. MARION O. CAUTHEN, MR. & MRS. J. DOUGLAS HOWELL, MR. & MRS. GLENN L. SCHRUM, H. L. HARGETT, JEAN R. HARGETT, MRS. MARTHA A. HUNT, DREW G. MIDDLETON, DOROTHY B. MIDDLETON, HENRY BAUCOM, JR., GLENDA C. BAUCOM, JERRY W. YORK, SUDIE J. YORK, MR. & MRS. W. T. BOWMAN, INDIVIDUALLY AND ON BEHALF OF ALL OTHER RESIDENTS OF THE DISTRICTS ZONED "RESIDENTIAL" AND ADJOINING AND LYING BETWEEN NEW DIXIE ROAD, AIRPORT DRIVE, MORRIS FIELD DRIVE AND TAGGART CREEK, IN MECKLENBURG COUNTY, WHO ARE SIMILARLY SITUATED v. QUEEN CITY SPEEDWAYS, INC.

No. 56

(Filed 30 January 1970)

1. Nuisance § 1— operation of motor vehicle speedway

While the operation of a motor vehicle speedway is a lawful enterprise and is therefore not a nuisance *per se*, it may, under varying circumstances, be a private nuisance *per accidens*.

2. Nuisance §§ 2, 7— operation of racetrack — violation of anti-noise ordinance

In this action to enjoin operation of a motor vehicle racetrack as a nuisance, the jury's verdict and court's findings of fact clearly show that defendant, by the operation of its racetrack, violated the terms of a municipal ordinance prohibiting in residential districts regularly recurring noises above a certain level from activities in adjoining business or industrial districts.

3. Nuisance § 1— violation of municipal ordinance

The mere violation of a municipal ordinance does not constitute a nuisance, but if the actual thing is a nuisance or in the nature thereof and it is done or maintained in violation of a municipal ordinance, it may constitute a nuisance against which relief may be obtained by one who suffers special and peculiar injury of an irreparable nature therefrom.

4. Nuisance §§ 2, 7— operation of motor vehicle racetrack — abatement of nuisance

In this action to enjoin the operation of a motor vehicle racetrack as a nuisance, wherein plaintiffs alleged and the jury by its verdict found that the noise of the racing vehicles on defendant's track was so loud as to cause plaintiffs discomfort and annoyance, to cause them to lose sleep at night, and to impair use and enjoyment of their homes, and that lights and dust from the racetrack, coupled with the noise, caused plaintiffs' property to depreciate in value and made their homes virtually uninhabitable while the races were in progress, the trial court erred in failing to abate the nuisance as found by the jury and in permitting defendant to continue operation of the racetrack under regulations imposed by the court.

BOBBITT, C.J., concurs in result.

Figure 5.1   Reprinted with the permission of LexisNexis.

42   N. C.   **172 SOUTH EASTERN REPORTER, 2d SERIES**

terrogation. Defendant Thorpe's inculpatory statement was admitted into evidence over objection. Holding that the statement was erroneously admitted, the Court stated:

> "*The Court, at the conclusion of the voir dire examination, did not make any findings with respect to counsel. The evidence before the Court was not sufficient to justify a finding that counsel at the interrogation was offered, or the defendant's right thereto was understandably waived.* In concluding the defendant was entitled to have counsel at his interrogation, and the right was not waived, we are no longer permitted to rely on the presumption that a confession is deemed to be voluntary until and unless the contrary is shown." (Emphasis ours)

The case of Carnley v. Cochran, 369 U.S. 506, 82 S.Ct. 884, 8 L.Ed.2d 70, presented the question of waiver of counsel where defendant was charged with a serious non-capital crime. The United States Supreme Court there said:

> "The record must show, or there must be an allegation and evidence which show, that an accused was offered counsel but intelligently and understandingly rejected the offer. Anything less is not waiver."

This quotation was approved in Miranda, v. Arizona, supra.

[4] These recent and well documented cases clearly stand for the rule that even in capital offenses a defendant may intelligently and understandingly waive counsel during an in-custody interrogation.

In the instant case there is plenary evidence in the record to support the conclusion of the trial judge that defendant McRae intelligently and understandingly waived counsel.

In the trial below we find

No error.

---

276 N.C. 231

Murle B. JONES et al.

v.

QUEEN CITY SPEEDWAYS, INC.

No. 56.

Supreme Court of North Carolina.

Jan. 30, 1970.

Action by nearby residents to enjoin the operation of a race track as a nuisance. The Superior Court, Mecklenburg County, Sam J. Ervin, III, J., entered a judgment permitting the continued operation of race track under regulations imposed by judgment and the plaintiffs appealed. On petition for certiorari case was certified for review before determination by Court of Appeals. The Supreme Court, Moore, J., held that where jury by its verdict found that defendant was operating its automobile race track in close proximity to numerous apartment houses in such a manner as to constitute a nuisance because of the lights, noise, and dust, plaintiffs were entitled to a judgment restraining operation of race track in the manner in which it caused nuisance, and court erred when it permitted defendant to continue operation under regulations imposed by judgment.

Error and remanded.

I. Nuisance ⬗3(9)

Operation of motor vehicle speedway is lawful enterprise and is not a nuisance per se, but under varying circumstances the operation may become a private nuisance *per accidens.*

2. Nuisance ⬗6, 26

Mere violation of municipal ordinance does not constitute a nuisance, but if actual thing is a nuisance or in nature thereof and is done or maintained in violation of ordinance, act may constitute such nuisance as against which relief may be obtained by one who suffers special and peculiar injury of irreparable nature therefrom.

Figure 5.2   Reprinted with the permission of West, a Thomson Business.

Opinion

Most opinions begin with a review of the procedural history of the case and the facts that brought the parties to court in the first place. If there are statutes which impact on the case, they are analyzed and applied to the facts at hand. Likewise, if other cases have previously addressed a similar conflict, they are reviewed and applied. Based upon these and other factors, including public policy and fairness, the court renders a decision. In so doing, it outlines its reasons. At the end of the case, you may find a dissenting opinion written by one or more of the judges who heard the case and disagree with the majority's decision. You may also find a concurring opinion in which one or more of the judges agrees with the majority's result, but disagrees with its reasoning.

As you read the opinion, occasionally you will see a number in brackets, printed in bold. These numbers refer back to the headnotes. Thus, if you read the first headnote at the beginning of the case, and it covers the question of whether an automobile racetrack is a nuisance, you can scan the opinion for the bold number 1 in brackets "[1]," and there you will find the portion of the opinion addressing this issue.

Finding Cases — Digests

There are many methods for finding cases on a particular topic. One excellent method is to use a digest. Digests are comprehensive subject-matter indexes to cases. They contain short summaries of reported cases, along with a citation giving you the name of the case, the court that decided it, and the date of the decision.

Figure 5.3 is a sample page from *West's North Carolina Digest, 2d*. Note the main topic at the top of the page: "Nuisances." Look for key number 3(9) and read the three summaries of two cases involving recetracks as nuisances.

For references to other topics, see Descriptive-Word Index

equity to interfere to enjoin the location of them near a dwelling.

> Ellison v. Commissioners of Town of Washington, 58 N.C. 57, 5 Jones Eq. 57, 75 Am.Dec. 430.

⊕~3(8). **Hospitals, asylums, and pesthouses.**

N.C. 1917. Pay hospital may become nuisance per se because of its location, or by reason of the manner in which it is conducted.

> Lawrence v. Nissen, 91 S.E. 1036, 173 N.C. 359.

⊕~3(9). **Games and entertainments.**

N.C. 1970. Operation of motor vehicle speedway is lawful enterprise and is not a nuisance per se, but under varying circumstances the operation may become a private nuisance per accidens.

> Jones v. Queen City Speedways, Inc., 172 S.E.2d 42, 276 N.C. 231.

N.C. 1965. A race track is not a nuisance per se but its operation may, under certain circumstances, be a "nuisance per accidens" or a nuisance in fact, as in a rural area.

> Hooks v. International Speedways, Inc., 140 S.E.2d 387, 263 N.C. 686.

Operation of prospective race track and injury flowing therefrom could be considered in determining whether to enjoin erection of race track and related structures.

> Hooks v. International Speedways, Inc., 140 S.E.2d 387, 263 N.C. 686.

⊕~3(10). **Keeping and slaughter of animals.**

N.C.App. 1970. Operation of a hog buying station is not a nuisance per se but may become a nuisance per accidens when improperly maintained or conducted.

> Moody v. Lundy Packing Co., 172 S.E.2d 905, 7 N.C.App. 463.

⊕~3(11). **Livery stables and garages.**

For other cases see the Decennial Digests and WESTLAW.

⊕~3(12). **Fences.**

N.C. 1963. A spite fence is a private nuisance.

> Welsh v. Todd, 133 S.E.2d 171, 260 N.C. 527.

A "spite fence" is one which is of no beneficial use to owner, and which is erected and maintained solely for purpose of annoying a neighbor.

> Welsh v. Todd, 133 S.E.2d 171, 260 N.C. 527.

N.C. 1941. A "spite fence", constituting nuisance, is one of no beneficial use to persons

erecting and maintaining it on their land solely for purpose of annoying owner of adjoining land.

> Burris v. Creech, 17 S.E.2d 123, 220 N.C. 302.

N.C. 1900. A barbed-wire fence negligently constructed and maintained on the edge of a pasture, dangerous through its location and construction and the probability of its causing injury to stock running in such pasture, constitutes a nuisance.

> Winkler v. Carolina & N.W. Ry. Co., 35 S.E. 621, 126 N.C. 370, 78 Am.St.Rep. 663.

N.C.App. 1997. Vendors did not plan to erect, out of spite, fence separating their property from adjacent land sold to purchasers, following purchasers' use of vendors' land to obtain access to building on purchasers' land; proposed fence met security needs of vendors, was of same chain link nature as perimeter fencing covering both properties, and did not deprive purchasers of light, air or view.

> Tedder v. Alford, 493 S.E.2d 487, 128 N.C.App. 27, review denied 501 S.E.2d 917, 348 N.C. 290.

⊕~4. **Nature and extent of injury or danger.**

Library references

C.J.S. Nuisances §§ 8, 13, 18, 19.

M.D.N.C. 1997. Under North Carolina law, to show interference sufficient to support claim for maintenance of private nuisance, landowner must prove substantial annoyance, material physical discomfort, or injury to health or property; touchstone is reasonableness where social utility of defendant's use is balanced against harm and interference with landowner's use of her property.

> Rudd v. Electrolux Corp., 982 F.Supp. 355.

Under North Carolina law, for landowner to show interference sufficient to support claim for maintenance of private nuisance, anticipated injuries must be more than conjectural and amount to actual interference with use and enjoyment of property; mere diminution in market value will not suffice.

> Rudd v. Electrolux Corp., 982 F.Supp. 355.

N.C. 1965. No one is justified in establishing, adjacent to a church, a business or amusement the noise of which will render practically impossible the continuance of customary religious services.

> Hooks v. International Speedways, Inc., 140 S.E.2d 387, 263 N.C. 686.

N.C. 1962. In order to render one liable for an intentional private nuisance per accidens,

Figure 5.3   Reprinted with the permission of West, a Thomson Business.

North Carolina cases can be found in *West's North Carolina Digest 2d*, *West's South Eastern Digest®*, and West's *American Digest System*. North Carolina cases can also be found through a series of books called *Strong's North Carolina Index*. *Strong's* looks a little different from a typical digest but can easily be used to find cases in much the same way as you would find them in a digest.

Coverage of Digests

There are lots of different digests. Which one you use depends upon how broadly you want to search. If you need only cases from a particular state, like North Carolina, then use a digest that includes only cases from that state, such as *West's North Carolina Digest, 2d*, or *Strong's North Carolina Index*. There are individual state digests for all the reported decisions from every state in the country.

If you need cases from a larger geographic area, you can use a regional digest that summarizes the decisions of several states in the same general geographic location. North Carolina cases are included in a regional digest called *West's South Eastern Digest, 2d®*. This digest, now in its second series, includes summaries of the cases in the South Eastern Reporter, including North Carolina, South Carolina, Georgia, Virginia, and West Virginia.

To broaden your search and find cases from across the country, you can use West's *American Digest System*: national digests including the decisions of both **state and federal courts,** divided into three parts:

(1) *Century Edition* — contains summaries of decisions from 1658–1896.
(2) *Decennial Digests* — contain summaries of decisions in ten-year groups from 1897 forward. The first group, cases from 1897–1906 is called the *First Decennial Digest*, the next group, cases from 1907–1916 is called the *Second Decennial Digest*, and so on. Beginning with the *Ninth Decennial Digest*, there are so many cases that the digest comes in two parts, *Part I* and *Part II*. *Part I* contains the first five years of the period, and *Part II*, the second five years.
(3) *General Digest* — contains summaries of the most recent cases. It operates much like an advance sheet, only bigger. It covers all the cases from the time the last *Decennial Digest* was completed, through the date of publication.

There are all sorts of other digests for particular kinds of cases as well. For example, West publishes a series of federal digests containing only federal cases. The most recent cases are in the *Federal Practice Digest, 4th*. Specialized digests summarize cases from particular courts, including bankruptcy, military justice, and Court of Claims. There are other specialized digests for particular subjects like computer law and construction law.

There are also two digests that deal only with the United States Supreme Court cases: the *United States Supreme Court Digest®* published by West, and the *U.S. Supreme Court Digest, Lawyer's Edition*, published by LexisNexis.

Digests published by West are organized by subject matter under the *key number* system. Each case is categorized by subject matter into one of the ±400 major topics, and then into one or more of the sub-topics within the major topic. For example, under the major topic, "Nuisance" you will find a series of sub-topics on various kinds of nuisances, including automobile racetracks at Nuisance, 3(9). Whether you are in the *North Carolina Digest*, a southeast regional digest, the national digest or some other digest, if it is published by West, then all the cases about whether a racetrack is a nuisance will be digested under that same topic and number: Nuisance 3(9).

Similarly, if you use another digest, you will again find all the cases grouped by topics, and in general, by sub-topics within those topics.

Finding Cases Using a Digest

Even though digests are essentially huge indexes to the law, the digests themselves have indexes. The best way to find a case on a particular topic is to start with the index to the digest. Consider the most likely words under which the case you seek might be indexed, and start there.

Descriptive-Word Index

When searching for a case on a particular topic, you will need a list of words to look up in the index to the digest that will help you find the cases on point. For example, assume that you have been asked to find cases addressing the issue of whether an automobile racetrack can be a "nuisance." To make a good list of indexing words, review the facts as you know them. Often, you will have been provided a written summary. If so, highlight or circle key words in the summary: "automobile," "racetrack," and "nuisance." These will be a good place to start in the index. Consider also who the parties are in the conflict, e.g., a "motor speedway" or a "neighborhood." This may provide you with a good indexing word or two. If this doesn't get you anywhere, try using words that describe where the events took place and what happened: residential neighborhood, racetrack, noise, traffic, cars, pollution, etc. Also consider the legal issue before you, e.g., "nuisance" or "tort," and any possible defenses. In theory, at least one of these words will lead you to the cases you need.

West's North Carolina Digest

Once you have a list of indexing words, find the appropriate digest. For North Carolina cases, use *West's® North Carolina Digest, 2d*. It is a series of red books with several index volumes at the end. Pick up the index to the digest and look up the most likely words on your list, such as "nuisance" or "racetrack" or "automobile." At least one of these *indexing words* will refer you to "Nuisance, Section 3(9)" and may refer you to other possible topics and key numbers also.

Once you have a reference from the index to the digest, go to the digest itself and look on the spines until you find the one that contains the topics you think are the most promising. For example, if you have chosen the topic, "Nuisance," look on the spine of the main volumes of the digest for the one containing topics starting with the letter "N." Leaf through the book and look for the word "nuisance" at the top of the page. When you find it, go to section 3, subsection (9).

When you open the digest to the topic of Nuisance, section 3(9) (or to any other topic), you will see a series of case summaries. Each is typically one sentence long, and describes a ruling by a particular court on the topic. It gives a few facts and a point of law. Also provided is a case name and citation.

For example, look at the sample digest page under "Nuisance" key number 3(9). The first entry begins, "**N.C. 1970.**" This tells you the case is from the North Carolina Supreme Court and was decided in 1970. (If it were from the North Carolina Court of Appeals, it would instead read, "N.C. App." like the first entry in "Nuisance" key number 3(10). And, if it were from a federal district court, it would read, "E.D.N.C.," "M.D.N.C.," or "W.D.N.C." and the year, like the entry under "Nuisance, key number 4.) Following the shorthand identification of the court and year of decision is the case summary. For example, the first entry under key number 3(9) indicates that a speedway is a lawful enterprise but can be a nuisance. Then, it reads, "*Jones v. Queen City Speedways, Inc.*, 172 S.E.2d 42, 2776 N.C. 231." This part tells you the name of the case ("*Jones v. Queen City Speedways, Inc.*") and gives you parallel citations to the two reporters where the case can be found: volume 172 of the S.E.2d, page 42, and volume 276 of the *North Carolina Reports*, page 686. Because the digest is a West product, it gives you the reference to the unofficial "S.E.2d" reporter first. You will have to reverse the order of the two reporters when you cite the case. (See Chapter 6.) Use these citations to find the entire opinion in a reporter.

Topic and Key Numbers

Once you have a useful topic and key number, you can use that number to access cases nationwide through West publications. You might acquire that topic and key number by using the digests themselves, or you might already have a case on point. If you already have a case, remember that the headnotes in the *South Eastern Reporter* provide the topic and key number of the pertinent points. You can use them to go straight to the digest volume containing that topic, whether a state, regional, or a national one, and find other cases on the same topic. Simply pick up the "N" volume and find Nuisance 3(9). Other cases may provide you with additional topics and key numbers that also relate to your case. Remember, however, that topics and key numbers only cross-reference within books published by West. If you are researching in the official reporters, the headnote topics and numbers will instead cross-reference you to *Strong's North Carolina Index*.

Strong's North Carolina Index

Strong's North Carolina Index is in wide use across the state. Although it doesn't look the same as a traditional digest, it can be used in a similar way. *Strong's* organizes the law by subject matter and summarizes it on each topic. Instead of publishing block summaries like those in a West digest, *Strong's* is written more like a textbook, using paragraph form. Each sentence, however, summarizes a different case (or statute), and is followed by a footnote number. The footnotes at the bottom of the page give you the case or statutory citation. Thus, much of the information is exactly the same as a digest—it just looks like a more typical reference book. However, in that *Strong's* also references statutes and other authorities, it is broader than a digest and more like an encyclopedia. And, because *Strong's* is now published by West, it also includes cross-references to key numbers and other West products.

Strong's is divided into hardbound main volumes, with supplementary pocket parts, followed by softbound indexes. The main volumes and the indexes are navy blue. There is also a separate *Archives Edition* containing older cases. Use the softbound indexes to help you find your way around. Start with a good list of indexing words. Look up the most likely words in the index, for references to the main volume. Or, if you already have a case in hand from the official reporter, use the headnote topics and reference numbers to take you to the relevant section of *Strong's*. Or, look up that case in *Strong's* case names index, for a reference to each section in *Strong's* where that case appears. There, you should find summaries of any other North Carolina cases on the same topic. Unless you need historical information, concentrate on the main volumes rather than the *Archive edition*.

Strong's only provides citations to cases and statutes from North Carolina. If you need to broaden your case search to a wider geographic region, switch to a regional or larger digest.

Exercise 5 — Finding and Reading Cases

Find each of the following cases and, (A) name the case; (B) provide its topic and key or section number; (C) list your finding words.

1. A 2002 case in the *North Carolina Digest* providing that in a sudden emergency, a person may be excused from liability for conduct that otherwise would be considered negligent.

    A.

    B.

    C.

2. A 1989 case against a doctor from the U.S. District Court for the Western District of North Carolina dealing with informed consent in a stomach stapling surgery.

    A.

    B.

    C.

3. An N.C. Supreme Court case in the *North Carolina Digest* where a prisoner was allowed to go to a movie, could not find his ride back to jail, and was later found guilty of escape.

    A.

    B.

    C.

    D. What was the year of decision?

    E. Was the case in the particular section you thought it should be? (If you cannot find the case in the most likely section, check sections nearby.)

4. A North Carolina case in the *North Carolina Digest* to the effect that a statute
    was constitutional when it provided that a person elected to fill a vacancy on
    the Superior Court or appellate courts serves only the remainder of the prior
    judge's term.

    A.

    B.

    C.

5. A 2002 North Carolina Court of Appeals case in the *North Carolina Digest* pro-
    viding that a holographic will (hand-written by the testator) including a phrase
    written with a different pen than the rest of the document did not render the
    will invalid.

    A.

    B.

    C.

6. A case in *Strong's North Carolina Index* providing that a city can regulate by
    zoning the location of a gas station pursuant to its general police power.

    A.

    B.

    C.

    D. What was the year of decision?

    E. Which court decided the case (Supreme Court or Court of Appeals)?

7. A case in *Strong's North Carolina Index* indicating that if an attorney professes
    to represent a particular client, it is presumed that he or she does so unless a
    person challenging that presumption is able to rebut it.

    A.

B.

C.

D. What was the year of decision?

E. Which court decided the case (Supreme Court or Court of Appeals)?

8. A 1998 case in *Strong's North Carolina Index* providing that the First Amend-
    ment does not grant religious organizations absolute immunity from tort lia-
    bility.

    A.

    B.

    C.

    D. What was the year of decision?

    E. Which court decided the case (Supreme Court or Court of Appeals)?

Chapter 6

Citing Cases

Required Elements

How do you cite a case? As always, begin with *The Bluebook*. Rule 10 governs citation of cases. Rule 10.1 and the *Bluepages* section B5 provide the basic elements in a citation and cross-references the rule specific to each element. The four essential elements of a case citation are the:

- name of the case, underlined or in italics (Rule 10.2);
- reporter(s) or other source of the case (Rule 10.3);
- court and jurisdiction that decided the case in parenthesis (including whether state or federal and whether trial court, court of appeals or supreme court) (Rule 10.4); and
- year the case was decided, in parentheses (Rule 10.5).

In addition, a full case citation should also include the relevant subsequent history of the case, describing the progress of the case through the courts after the date of the cited decision. It is also possible to include additional information in a case cite, but rarely is this necessary.

Name of the Case—Rule 10.2

Reporters and court opinions typically set out the complete case name, including the full names of all the parties on all sides of the conflict. In a case **citation**, your job is to reduce the full case name to a manageable size, while still enabling anyone who reads your cite to find it with ease. Many people simply use the shortened version of the name that appears in the reporter at the top of each page of the case. Although not always technically correct under *The Bluebook* rules, this version of the case name is often sufficient or can be made so with minor revisions in accordance with Rule 10.2 in *The Bluebook*.

Of course, there will be times when your citation needs to be exactly and technically correct. In those situations, follow the detailed requirements of Rule 10.2. Once you have learned the Rule, you can relax your standards, depending upon the context in which you are citing cases.

No matter how you shorten the name, be sure to always put the case name in italics, or underline it.

Textual Sentences vs. Stand-Alone Citations

When citing a case name, the *Bluebook* requirements vary, depending on whether you are citing the case as part of a textual sentence or as a separate, stand-alone citation. A cite in a textual sentence is one where the citation is included within a sentence in your document:

> In *Jones v. Queen City Speedways, Inc.*, 276 N.C. 231, 172 S.E.2d 42 (1965), the court ruled that the plaintiffs' allegations were sufficient to support a finding against the defendant racetrack for nuisance.

A stand-alone citation is its own, separate sentence:

> The Supreme Court has ruled that the presence of a racetrack near a residential neighborhood can be a nuisance. *Jones v. Queen City Speedways, Inc.*, 276 N.C. 231, 172 S.E.2d 42 (1965).

Shortening All Case Names

All case names must be shortened from their full version. The names included in citations that are part of a textual sentence must be shortened in accordance with Rule 10.2.1. If your citation is a stand-alone sentence, further shorten the case name according to Rule 10.2.2. In general, it is best to start with the full name, and then go through the rules to see what you can omit.

For example, the full name of the case cited above (as set out in the official reporter) is:

> *Murle B. Jones, Mary H. Jones, George W. Jones, Eddie B. Jones, Thomas G. Ginn, Virginia P. Ginn, Mr. & Mrs. Roger D. Ginn, W. Jack Wingate, Pearl D. Wingate, L. P. Wofford, Gwendolyn B. Wofford, Mr. & Mrs. Marion O. Cauthen, Mr. & Mrs. J. Douglas Howell, Mr. & Mrs. Glenn L. Schrum, H. L. Hargett, Jean R. Hargett, Mrs. Martha A. Hunt, Drew G. Middleton, Dorothy B. Middleton, Henry Baucom, Jr., Glenda C. Baucom, Jerry W. York, Sudie J. York, Mr. & Mrs. W. T. Bowman, individually, and on behalf of all other residents of the districts zoned "residential" and adjoining and lying between New Dixie Road, Airport Drive, Morris Field Drive and Taggart Creek, in Mecklenburg County, who are similarly situated v. Queen City Speedways, Inc.*

As you can imagine, if you had to include all those names and descriptions in your document every time you cited that case, it would take up a lot of space and require an inordinate amount of typing. The *Bluebook* rules allow omission of much of the information in the name. Each subsection of Rule 10.2.1 addresses different issues that may arise in a case name, and includes examples of both what to do, and what not to do.

Rule 10.2.1(a) provides that when a case involves **two or more actions** that have been consolidated, you need only cite the first action. Thus, if the case is *A v. B* *and X v. Y*, you can omit "*and X v. Y*" from your citation. Further, you may **omit all the parties in the case except the first party listed on each side.** In accordance with this part of the rule, in the racetrack case name set out above you can omit all the parties' names except the first one on each side. Thus, what began as a very long name is reduced to, "*Murle B. Jones v. Queen City Speedways, Inc.*" (It will be shortened even more when other parts of Rule 10 are applied.) Even though there are in fact multiple parties, don't use words like "*et al.*" (meaning "and others") and don't use alternative names, like "d/b/a's." Already, you have saved considerable space and time.

Rule 10.2.1(b) requires that you abbreviate the following and similar phrases to "*ex rel*":

- *on the relation of*
- *for the use of*
- *on behalf of*
- *as next friend of.*

Abbreviate these and similar phrases to "*In re*":

- *in the matter of*
- *petition of*
- *application of.*

According to **Rule 10.2.1(c)**, the following **eight words can always be abbreviated** as shown, unless they are the first word in either party's name:

- and: &
- Association: Ass'n
- Brothers: Bros.
- Company: Co.
- Corporation: Corp.
- Incorporated: Inc.
- Limited: Ltd.
- Number: No.

Note that some of the required abbreviations employ apostrophes in place of missing letters ("Ass'n"), and others require periods ("Bros.").

In addition, **commonly known acronyms** can also be abbreviated, such as "NAACP" or "NLRB." If you're unsure how commonly known an acronym might be, don't abbreviate it.

In stand-alone citations, you must also abbreviate a host of **additional words listed in table T.6.** Again, pay attention to the placement of periods versus apostrophes. For example, "Assoc." is the abbreviation for "Associate" according to the Table, while "Ass'n" is the abbreviation for "Association." Add an "s" inside any period if the word is plural. Thus, "Associates" becomes "Assocs." and "Associations" becomes "Ass'ns" in accordance with the opening paragraph of the table.

Under **Rule 10.2.1(d)**, **omit "The"** as the first word of a party's name unless royalty is involved or "The" is part of a popular name.

Omit **descriptive terms** per **Rule 10.2.1(e)**, including "administrator," "appellee," "executor," "licensee," and "trustee" if they follow a comma (e.g., "Smith, Appellee" becomes just "Smith" but "Trustees of Dartmouth College," does not become just "Dartmouth College" because the descriptive word ("Trustees") does not follow a comma.

Rule 10.2.1(f), dealing with **geographic terms**, often applies. For instance, this rule deals with circumstances where the state is a party, as it is in criminal cases. It requires that you omit words like "State of" from your citation unless you are citing a decision of that state, in which case, only "State" or a similar word should be used. Applying this rule to North Carolina criminal case decisions, *State of North Carolina v. Jones* will become *State v. Jones*. But, if the case leaves the North Carolina court system and is decided by another court, like the United States Supreme Court, then the case name will read, *North Carolina v. Jones*. The difference is in the deciding court. So long as the case is in a North Carolina court, the name includes only the word "State." But if the case involves North Carolina and is heard in an out-of-state or federal court, it will be "North Carolina" instead.

Rule 10.2.1(f) requires omissions of "City of" from the case name unless it begins a party name. Thus, if the case name were, "Mayor of the City of New York v. Clinton," you would omit "the City of," leaving you with "Mayor of New York." But, if the case name began, "City of New York v. Clinton," you would keep "City of" because it begins that party's name.

Similarly, you can typically omit all "prepositional phrases of location" unless, (1) the phrase follows the word "City"; (2) the omission of the phrase would leave only one word in the name of the party; or (3) the location is part of the name of a business. (Prepositions include words like "of," "on," "in" and "by.") So, as described immediately above, keep "City of New York," even though "of New York" is a prepositional phrase of location, because it follows "City of," and omitting it would leave you with only one word in the name of the party. But as exemplified in *The Bluebook*:

> *Surrick v. Board of Wardens*
> **Not:** *Surrick v. Board of Wardens of the Port of Philadelphia*[1]

Here, "of the Port of Philadelphia" is a prepositional phrase of location (note the preposition "of") and can be omitted, since it still leaves more than one word in that party's name. On the other hand, you must keep "of Harrisburg" in *Shapiro v. Bank of Harrisburg*, and "of Omaha" in *Elmers v. Mutual of Omaha*, because otherwise the name of the party would be only one word long, and also because "Bank of Harrisburg" and "Mutual of Omaha" are the names of businesses.

Finally, omit "*of America*" after "United States." Retain all geographic designations not introduced by a preposition.

---

1. *The Bluebook: A Uniform System of Citation* R. 10.2.1(f), at 60 (Columbia Law Review Ass'n et al. Eds., 17th ed. 2000).

Rule 10.2.1(g) requires that you **omit given names**. Thus, our citation can be further shortened from *Murle B. Jones v. Queen City Speedways, Inc.* to *Jones v. Queen City Speedways, Inc.* Be careful with this part of the rule. When a given name is included in a company name, you must keep it. For instance, if Gloria Vanderbilt sues Mr. X in her own name, the case caption would read, "*Vanderbilt v. X.*" But, if Gloria Vanderbilt, Inc., sues Mr. X, the case caption would read, "*Gloria Vanderbilt, Inc. v. X.*"

Business firm designations like "Inc." or "LLC" can be omitted if the name already includes another business designation, so that it is clear that the party is an entity, not a person. See **Rule 10.2.1(h)**. For example, *Legal Research Company, Inc.* becomes *Legal Research Co.* in accordance with subsection (h) (omit "Inc.") and subsection (c)) (shorten "Company" to "Co.").

Unions and the Commissioner of Revenue are covered by **Rules 10.2.1(i)** and (j) respectively.

If your citation stands alone as a separate sentence, Rule 10.2.2. provides that you must abbreviate all the words set out in table T.6. In stand-alone citations, also abbreviate states, countries, and other geographical units that are included in a case name in accordance with table T.11 if that state or country is not a party. If the geographical unit is a party, don't abbreviate, but refer back to **Rule 10.2.1(f)** concerning geographical terms.

Practice Set 6.1

Shorten the following case names in accordance with *Bluebook* rules 10.2.1. and 10.2.2:

1. *Claude Hooks, A.G. Goins, D. J. Powell, D. J. Shelly, Elwood Robinson, Mickey Long, Cecil Gurkin, H.H. Collins, Henry Merritt, Luther High, and Daniel M. Spell, Officers and Trustees of Smyrna Baptist Church v. International Speedways, Incorporated and Marie D. Carter*

2. *Texaco, Inc., Petitioner v. Ricky Hasbrouck, dba Rick's Texaco, et al.*

3. *State of North Carolina, Plaintiff-Appellee/Cross Appellant v. Daniel J. Krim, Defendant-Appellant/Cross Appellee.* (Assume this case was decided in North Carolina.)

4. *In re the Estate of Lois v. Greenheck, Deceased*

5. *Chase Bryant and Charles Bryant v. Independent School District No. 1-38 of Great County, North Carolina, a.k.a. Reallygood Public Schools*

Source of the Case: Reporters—Rule 10.3

The next part of the citation after the case name is the identification of the reporter(s) in which the case appears. This may also identify for your reader the court and jurisdiction of the case, in accordance with Rule 10.4, depending upon how you set up the citation.

Citations to cases in reporters must identify the volume number in which the case appears, the abbreviated name of the reporter in accordance with table T.1, and the page on which it begins—in that order, e.g., "276 N.C. 231." Here, "276" is the volume number, "N.C." identifies the North Carolina Supreme Court Reports (and hence the court), and "231" is the page number on which the case begins.

Citations to North Carolina Cases

Every case from the North Carolina appellate courts will be reported in at least two reporters: an official reporter (either the *North Carolina Supreme Court Reports* or the *North Carolina Court of Appeals Reports*) and the *South Eastern Reporter* (either the original or the second series). In accordance with *Bluebook* rules, you must always give the cite to the unofficial regional reporter (the *South Eastern Reporter*). The general practice in North Carolina is to include both reporters in one citation, i.e. to give parallel cites.

Parallel Cites

Parallel cites are references to both the official and unofficial reporter in the same citation. For example, the citation, *Jones v. Queen City Speedways, Inc.*, 276 N.C. 231, 172 S.E.2d 42 (1970), includes parallel cites: the first to the case in the official reporter, and the second to the case in the unofficial regional reporter. That same citation, without parallel cites, would instead look like this: *Jones v. Queen City Speedways, Inc.*, 172 S.E.2d 42 (N.C. 1970). In both cites, the reference to the unofficial S.E.2d reporter appears.

Which way should you cite? The *Bluepages* require that,

> In documents submitted to state courts, all citations to cases should be to the reporters required by **local rules**. To find the local rules for the court in which you are submitting a document, refer to Bluepages table BT.2.[2]

In North Carolina, the convention is to use parallel citations. Further, parallel citations appear to be contemplated by the North Carolina Rules of Appellate Procedure, which include them in sample case citations in a table of cases.

When giving parallel cites, the official reporter is always cited first, followed by the unofficial West regional reporter.

To determine how to abbreviate the official and unofficial reporters, look at *table T.1* for North Carolina. The first entry is for the North Carolina Supreme Court.

---

2. *Id.* B5.1.3 at 9.

(Note that the rule says, "Cite to S.E. or S.E.2d, if therein; otherwise cite to N.C."[3] Even so, because the convention is to use parallel cites in North Carolina, ignore this directive unless you are instructed otherwise.) Under the bold heading "**Supreme Court**" are listed all the reporters where North Carolina Supreme Court case opinions can be found, and the dates covered by each reporter. According to the list, you can cite Supreme Court cases from the latter half of the 1800s forward to the official *North Carolina Reports* ("N.C.") and the unofficial *South Eastern Reporter* ("S.E." or "S.E.2d" depending upon the date).

For example, the Jones v. Queen City Speedways, Inc., case is published in volume 276 of the *North Carolina Reports* beginning on page 231. The case therefore would be cited from the official reporter as: "276 N.C. 231." Here, the information about the reporter also identifies the court and jurisdiction: the abbreviated name of the reporter, "N.C." also indicates that this is a case from the North Carolina Supreme Court.

That same case also appears in volume 172 of the *South Eastern Reporter, 2nd Series*, beginning on page 42. It would be cited in that volume as: "172 S.E.2d 42." (Note that "S.E.2d has no spaces.) Putting the cite together, then, using parallel citations, the case would be cited as, Jones v. Queen City Speedways, Inc., 276 N.C. 231, 172 S.E.2d 42 (1970). Note the structure of the citation: case name (underlined or in italics), official reporter including volume and page number, unofficial reporter including volume and page number, and year of decision in parentheses.

Sample citation to a related case from the North Carolina Supreme Court using parallel cites:

Hooks v. International Speedways, Inc., 263 N.C. 686, 140 S.E.2d 387 (1965).

A case from the North Carolina Court of Appeals is cited in much the same way. If you are using parallel cites, after the name, give the citation to the official reporter. Because it is a Court of Appeals case, the official reporter is identified as "N.C. App."[4] Don't cite the *North Carolina Court of Appeals Reports* as "N.C. Ct. App." That is the abbreviation for the Court of Appeals itself. Instead, look down the list of reporters in Table T.1 (in this case there are only two) and find the right abbreviation: "N.C. App." Note the space between "N.C." and "App."

When citing a North Carolina Court of Appeals case, give the citation to the official reporter first. According to the list under **Court of Appeals** in table T.1, all Court of Appeals cases appear in the S.E.2d (never in the S.E.). This is because the Court of Appeals was created after the *South Eastern Reporter* was already in its second series.

---

3. *The Bluebook: A Uniform System of Citation* T. 1, at 224 (Columbia Law Review Ass'n et al. Eds., 18th ed. 2005).
    4. *Id.* T.1 at 225.

> Sample citation to a case from the North Carolina Court of Appeals using parallel cites:
>
> *Sides v. Duke Univ.*, 74 N.C. App. 331, 328 S.E.2d 818 (1985)

Finding Parallel Citations

Often, the resource that led you to the case you are citing will have provided you with the parallel cites. For example, both the *West's North Carolina Digest* and *Strong's North Carolina Index* typically include a citation to both the official N.C. or N.C. App. reporter, and to the unofficial S.E. or S.E.2d. If you find the case through a secondary source, there is an excellent chance both citations will be provided. However, from time to time you will find yourself with one of the two citations and not the other. There are a variety of means for obtaining the parallel citation.

Perhaps the easiest method of finding the other half of a parallel cite is via **Lexis** or **Westlaw**, two widely-used computer-assisted legal research services. Go to the function that allows you to "get a document" and type in the part of the citation you have. For example, if you know the case you want is printed at 310 N.C. 312, simply type that in. The service will pull up the case for you and give you a citation to any other reporter in which it is printed. Thus, you will find that this particular case is available at 310 N.C. 312, 312 S.E.2d 405, and at 57 A.L.R. 4th 1. In addition, it will provide you with the citation for that case on that service, e.g. 1984 N.C. LEXIS 1576. Of course, you do not need all these citations in your parallel cite. Stick with *The Bluebook* requirements and cite the official reporter and the unofficial West reporter only. Thus, the case mentioned above would be cited as:

Renwick v. News and Observer, 310 N.C. 312, 312 S.E.2d 405 (1984).

Note that no A.L.R, Lexis, or Westlaw cite is included, even though each is available.

Many people do not have access to computer-assisted legal research. And, it is expensive. Fortunately, you can find parallel citations through books instead. For North Carolina, West publishes a **North Carolina Blue and White Book**. This single volume gives you parallel citations for both the official and West reporters. Half of the book is on blue paper, and the other half is on white. If you have an official citation, whether to "N.C." or N.C. App.", go to the blue pages. Look up your cite first by volume, then page, and you will be provided with the volume and page number where that case appears in the S.E. or S.E.2d.

For example, if you know that *Renwick v. News and Observer* is located at 310 N.C. 312, but don't know where it is in the *Southeastern Reporter*, you can go to the listing for volume 310 of the "N.C." reporter, page 312, on the blue pages. (Be sure you are in the *North Carolina Reports* section rather than the *North Carolina Court of Appeals Reports*.) You will see the parallel cite is 312 S.E.2d 405. Similarly, if you have the citation to the case in the S.E. or S.E.2d (e.g. 312 S.E.2d 405), go to the white pages, and find the volume number 312 and page 405. You will be provided with the official reporter citation.

The *North Carolina Blue and White Book* is supplemented as needed, to provide parallel citations to more recent cases.

The same blue pages as appear in the *North Carolina Blue and White Book* are reprinted in the front of some volumes of the *South Eastern Reporter*. If you have them in your library, you may be able to get the parallel cites to the official reporter there. The spines of the books tell you which cases are covered on the blue pages within.

Another means of finding a parallel citation is through *Shepard's North Carolina Case Name Citator* or *Shepard's Citations,* both referred to by practitioners as *"Shepard's."* The easier of the two is **Shepard's North Carolina Case Name Citator**. Simply look up the name of the case, and you will find its citation in both the official and unofficial reporter, along with the year of decision. Do be careful if you are looking up a case with a common name. For example, there are many North Carolina decisions captioned *"State v. Smith."* Presumably, you will have at least half the citation. Match that up to a case in the citator to find the right parallel cite.

You may instead use **Shepard's Citations**. This is a multi-volume set, so your first task will be to pick up the correct volumes. There are several bound volumes that cover cases, and of course, supplements for cases printed after the bound volumes came out. Find the most recent supplement and look for the box on its cover titled, "What your library should contain." Assemble all the books listed there. These will include four 1995 hardbound volumes numbered 1–4, a hardbound 1995–2000 supplement, a gold soft cover supplement, and a red soft cover supplement. Start with the 1995 volumes and look on their spines to see whether they contain information on cases from the *North Carolina Reports, Court of Appeals Reports, South Eastern Reporter,* or *South Eastern Reporter, Second Series.* Choose the one that matches the citation you have.

Assume that you have in your hand the official version of *Renwick v. News and Observer,* so you know that it is published in 310 N.C. 312. Assume further that you do not know the parallel citation for the *Southeastern Reporter.* Look for the volumes of *Shepard's Citations* which include cases from the official North Carolina Supreme Court reporter ("N.C."). Then look specifically for the volume of *Shepard's* which includes cases from volume 310 of the N.C. reporter, and open it to the section covering North Carolina Supreme Court cases. Use the header at the top of the page to make sure you are in the right place. It should say, "NORTH CAROLINA REPORTS." On the outer corner of each page, you will see a volume number. This corresponds to the volume number of the reporter you are looking up. Find volume 310 in the upper corner of the page. (It should be on page 595 of the hardbound *Shepard's* volume you are using, if you are in the 1995 volume.) Then scan the columns until you see "312" (the page number of the case) in bold. Immediately under the bold "— 312 —" you will see the name and year of the case: "Renwick v. News and Observer Publishing Co. 1984." (See Figure 10.1 in Chapter 10 for a copy of the page described here.)

Immediately below the case name, in parentheses, you will see, "(312SE405)." Next, also in parentheses, you will see "(57ALl1)." Thereafter, you will see a long column of numbers and letters. (Those will be covered in chapter 10, on *Shepard's Citations*.) **The two sets of numbers and letters in parentheses are parallel cites to the *Renwick* case.** The first is a short-hand version of "312 S.E.2d 405," the parallel cite to the case in the *Southeastern Reporter, Second Series*. The other is to the A.L.R. 4th ("*American Law Reports*"), a legal resource that includes reprints of important cases.

Using *Shepard's Citations* is perhaps the most complicated means of obtaining the parallel cite. However, after you have learned to use *Shepard's* more thoroughly (see Chapter 10), using it to find parallel cites won't seem as difficult.

Citations to North Carolina Cases without Parallel Cites

In most circumstances in North Carolina, you will use parallel cites. However, some states' cases are available in only one reporter. If so, the reporter will likely be a West product. Although it is not yet so in North Carolina, there may be a national trend toward citing just the West regional reporter, as exemplified by the *Bluebook's* directive in table T.1 for both the Supreme Court and Court of Appeals. The table says "Cite to S.E. or S.E.2d, if therein."[5] Remember, this directive pertains only when you are not required to give parallel citations. You may then limit your citation to just the volume and page of the S.E. or S.E.2d. However, in that case, you will have to add information to your date parenthetical, explaining from which court and jurisdiction the case comes.

Consider the following incomplete citation: <u>Hooks v. International Speedways, Inc.</u>, 140 S.E.2d 387 (1965). Here, in accordance with *The Bluebook*, T.1, the case is cited only to the S.E.2d. Remember, though, *Bluebook* Rule 10 requires that every case citation identify the court and jurisdiction (see *Bluebook* Rule 10.1 and 10.4). Can you tell what level of court decided the <u>Hooks</u> case from the information provided here (Court of Appeals vs. Supreme Court)? Can you tell what state (jurisdiction) decided the case? The answer to both questions is, no. There is nothing to indicate whether the decision came from a Supreme Court or Court of Appeals. Nor can you determine the jurisdiction. You can only surmise that it was an appellate decision from one of the five states in the South East region: North Carolina, South Carolina, Georgia, Virginia, or West Virginia.

To correct this lack of information, when citing only to an unofficial regional reporter, add the court and jurisdiction inside the date parenthetical. For North Carolina, this can be accomplished easily. If the case comes from the North Carolina Supreme Court, add "N.C." just before the year of the decision. "N.C." is the appropriate identifier of the North Carolina Supreme Court as set out in table T.1 (in parentheses just after the bold "**Supreme Court**" heading). If the case comes from the North Carolina Court of Appeals, add "N.C. Ct. App."—the identifier of the Court of Appeals according to the parenthetical immediately following the bold heading "**Court of Appeals**" in table T.1. Do not use "N.C. App." in the parentheti-

---

5. Id. T.1, at 224.

cal if you are citing only the *South Eastern Reporter*. "N.C. App." is the abbreviation for the *North Carolina Court of Appeals Reports*. "N.C. Ct. App." is the abbreviation for the North Carolina Court of Appeals itself.

Sample citation to a case from the N.C. Supreme Court using only the regional reporter:

> *Hooks v. International Speedways, Inc.*, 140 S.E.2d 387 (N.C. 1965).

* * *

Sample citation to a case from the N.C. Court of Appeals using only the regional reporter:

> *Sides v. Duke Univ.*, 328 S.E.2d 818 (N.C. Ct. App. 1985)

Review the foregoing examples. Now can you tell what level of court each case is from by looking at the date parenthetical? Can you also tell what state decided each case? Of course, you can. The "N.C." in the Hooks citation identifies the North Carolina Supreme Court, and the N.C. Ct. App. in the Sides citation identifies the North Carolina Court of Appeals. Thus, these citations satisfy the requirements of *The Bluebook* without using parallel cites.

Practice Set 6.2

1. Cite <u>Renwick v. News and Observer</u>, 310 N.C. 312, 312 S.E.2d 405 (1984) in *Bluebook* form but without using parallel cites.

2. Cite the case <u>In re Dixon</u> in *Bluebook* form. It was decided in 1993 and appears in volume 112 of the North Carolina Court of Appeals reporter on page 248, and in volume 435 of the *South Eastern Reporter, 2d Series* on page 352.

   A) With parallel cites:

   B) Without parallel cites:

3. Cite the case of <u>State v. Smith</u> in *Bluebook* form. It was decided in 1953 and appears in volume 73 of the *South Eastern Reporter, 2d Series* on page 901, and in volume 236 of the *Supreme Court Reports* on page 748.

   A) With parallel cites:

   B) Without parallel cites:

Date or Year — Rule 10.5

The last required element in a case citation is the date or year of decision. This is always placed inside parentheses at the end of the citation. You can find the date of decision at the beginning of each court opinion, immediately after the case caption. Be sure to cite the date of the opinion, not the date the reporter was published.

Citing Federal Cases

Citations to federal cases require the same elements as citations to state court cases:

- the name (underlined or in italics),
- the source (reporter) where the case can be found including volume and page number,
- the court and jurisdiction, and
- the year of decision in parentheses at the end.

Again, table T.1 provides the information you need for each federal court and the reporters that print their decisions. The federal court listings are at the very beginning of T.1.

United States Supreme Court Case Citations

According to *The Bluebook's* table T.1, U.S. Supreme Court cases are cited to "U.S. if therein; otherwise cite to the S. Ct., L. Ed., or U.S.L.W. in that order of preference."[6] Each of those four sources is then listed, giving you its official name, the dates it covers, and its correct abbreviation. Pay attention to upper and lower case lettering and to spacing. "U.S." means the official *United States Reports*. "S. Ct." stands for the *Supreme Court Reporter*, an unofficial reporter published by West. "L. Ed." stands for *Lawyer's Edition*, another unofficial reporter, now owned by LexisNexis®. It is available in an original ("L. Ed.") and a second series ("L. Ed. 2d"). And, "U.S.L.W." stands for *United States Law Week*, yet another unofficial reporter of Supreme Court cases. Whichever publisher you choose, you will find the exact same opinion, word for word. However, the volume and page numbers will be different, as will be the headnotes, annotations and other references.

The Bluebook in table T.1 anticipates that you will cite only the official reporter and not give parallel citations. However, sometimes you will be asked to give parallel cites anyway. If so, give the first three unless instructed otherwise: the official re-

---

6. *The Bluebook* T.1 at 193.

porter ("U.S.") and the first two unofficial reporters ("S. Ct." and "L. Ed." or "L. Ed. 2d"), in that order. For each one, give the volume number, the abbreviated name of the reporter, and the page number on which the case begins in that reporter.

Sample citation to a case from the U.S. Supreme Court using only the official reporter:

Roe v. Wade, 410 U.S. 113 (1973)

* * *

Sample citation to a case from the U.S. Supreme Court using parallel citations:
Roe v. Wade, 410 U.S. 113, 93 S. Ct. 705, 35 L. Ed. 2d 147 (1973)

United States Court of Appeals Case Citations

Cases from the United States Courts of Appeals are published in the *Federal Reporter* published by West. Do not cite any parallel reporter. Depending upon the year of decision, the case may appear in the original series of the *Federal Reporter* ("F."), the second series ("F.2d") or in the most recent third series ("F.3d"). Note that there is no space between "F." and "2d." or "3d."

When citing a case to the *Federal Reporter*, you must identify the court and jurisdiction within the parentheses containing the date. Otherwise, your citation will not indicate which U.S. Court of Appeals heard the case. Federal cases from North Carolina are heard in the Fourth Circuit of the United States Court of Appeals. This is abbreviated as "4th Cir." Including the numbered circuit inside the parentheses is sufficient to satisfy the requirements of the rule.

Sample citation to a case from the U.S. Court of Appeals, Fourth Circuit:

Belk v. Charlotte-Mecklenburg Board of Education, 233 F.3d 232 (4th Cir. 2000)

Practice Set 6.3

1. Cite the case of Home Port Rentals, Inc. v. Ruben, from the Fourth Circuit in 1992. The case is reported in volume 957 of the *Federal Reporter, 2d Series* starting on page 126.

   _____

2. Cite the 2003 Fourth Circuit decision in United States v. Hylton, appearing on page 781 of the *Federal Reporter, 3d Series*, volume 349.

   _____

United States District Court Case Citations

The decisions of the United States District Courts (the federal trial courts) are published primarily in the *Federal Supplement* ("F. Supp.") or in its second series ("F. Supp. 2d"). Some appear in the *Federal Rules Decisions* ("F.R.D.") or the *Bankruptcy Reporter* ("B.R.") or another specialized federal reporter. The various federal reporters are all listed in *The Bluebook* table T.1, after the United States Courts of Appeals and other specialized federal appellate courts. For the most part, you will cite to the *Federal Supplement.*

Because citing the *Federal Supplement* does not identify the court and jurisdiction, you must add this information to the parentheses with the date. For District Court cases, this means you must identify the particular district court whose decision you are citing. The three North Carolina federal district courts are the Eastern, Middle, and Western. They are abbreviated "E.D.N.C.," "M.D.N.C.," and "W.D.N.C.," respectively.

Sample citation to a case from the U.S. District Court, Eastern District:

Fulbright v. Apfel, 114 F. Supp. 2d 465 (W.D.N.C. 2000)

In all your federal citations, remember to space and capitalize your abbreviations for the courts and jurisdictions just as *The Bluebook* does. For example, "E.D. N.C." is wrong, while "E.D.N.C." is right. (On the other hand, "D. Mass." is right but "D.Mass." is wrong. Typically, *The Bluebook* requires a space before any state abbreviation that includes both upper and lower case letters.)

Practice Set 6.4

1. Cite the case appearing on page 293 of the Federal Supplement, volume 759, entitled, "Haburjack v. Prudential Bache Securities, Inc." It was decided in 1991 and came from the Western District of North Carolina.

    _____

2. Cite the case of Swain Island Club, Inc. v. White, coming out of the Eastern District of North Carolina in 1953, and appearing in volume 114 of the Federal Supplement on page 95.

    _____

Subsequent History — Rule 10.7

Cases ordinarily work their way through the court system beginning with the trial court, then the Court of Appeals, and finally the Supreme Court. Typically, you will cite the opinion of the highest court that last considered the case. Occasionally, however, you may want to cite a lower court's opinion, even though the case was considered later by a higher court. This occurs most often when the higher court affirms the decision you are citing without comment, or when it declines to hear the case at all, leaving the decision you are citing as the final word on the matter. Opinions written after the one you are citing concerning the same case are known as "subsequent history."

According to Rule 10.7, you must include the subsequent history of a case whenever you are giving a full citation. You may omit denials of certiorari or other discretionary appeals (where the higher court declines to hear the case) if the decision you are citing is more than two years old, unless the denial is particularly relevant (a subjective determination). In general, you can end your recitation of a case's subsequent history with any remand of the case back to the trial court. And, you can omit any denials of a rehearing, unless it is "particularly relevant."

To add subsequent history to a citation, add a comma at the end of the citation of the case, then add the appropriate explanatory phrase describing what the higher court did, either underlined, or in italics, followed by another comma. The commonly used explanatory phrases are set out in table T.8. Use the abbreviations shown. Some of the most commonly used are:

- *aff'd*: the higher court affirmed (agreed with) the decision of the lower court;
- *rev'd*: the higher court reversed (overturned) the decision of the lower court;
- *modified*: the higher court modified (changed) the decision of the lower court;
- *cert. denied*: the higher court denied certiorari (refused to take up the case);
- *reh'g denied*: the higher court refused to rehear (reconsider) its own decision in the case.

After the abbreviated explanatory phrase and comma, give the volume, reporter and page number on which the subsequent case opinion appears, followed by the date of the later opinion in parentheses. Be sure to include the court and jurisdiction in the date parenthetical of your subsequent history unless you are using parallel citations.

Examples of subsequent history in a case citations:

Tedder v. Alford, 128 N.C. App. 27, 493 S.E.2d 487 (1997), *review denied*, 348 N.C. 290, 501 S.E.2d 917 (1998)

Swain Island Club, Inc. v. White, 114 F. Supp. 95 (E.D.N.C. 1953), *aff'd*, 209 F.2d 698 (4th Cir. 1954)

Exercise 6 — Citing Cases

Cite the following cases using parallel cites unless directed otherwise. Abbreviate the case names as stand-alone citations. Include any subsequent history in accordance with Rule 10.7, and give all parallel citations to the United States Supreme Court cases to the official and first two unofficial reporters.

1. The case appearing in volume 169 of the *North Carolina Reports* on page 584.

   Cite this case without parallel citations, in *Bluebook* form.

2. The case involving Emerald Isle Realty in volume 350 of the *North Carolina Reports*.

3. The case appearing on page 349 of the *South Eastern Reporter, Second Series*, volume 23.

4. The case involving the State of North Carolina and Robbins, from volume 356 of the S.E.2d.

5. The case on page 397 of the *North Carolina Reports*, volume 208.

6. A 1955 N.C. Supreme Court case holding that the unauthorized removal of a dead body from a grave is an indictable offense. (Use the *North Carolina Digest* or *Strong's.*]

7. A divorce case involving the Wades reported on page 372, volume 72, of the *North Carolina Court of Appeals Reports*.

   Cite this case without parallel citations, in *Bluebook* form.

8. A case from volume 89 of the *North Carolina Court of Appeals Reports* involving the question of whether a tenant is entitled to a rent abatement due to a defective water heater in her apartment. (Use the *Words & Phrases* or *Analytical Index* in the reporter.)

9. A case from volume 171 of the *Federal Reporter, 3d Series*, beginning on page 939.

10. A case involving Monroe Hardware Company from volume 621 of the *Federal Supplement*.

Chapter 7

Briefing Cases

Elements of a Case Brief

As a legal professional, you may be called upon to brief cases, that is, to summarize the important elements of a court opinion in a particular style and format. Attorneys differ on the particular style they prefer. In general, however, a case brief will mirror the components of the court opinion itself, in approximately the following order:

(1) Case Caption;
(2) Facts;
(3) Procedural History;
(4) Issue;
(5) Holding;
(6) Reasoning;
(7) Judgment;
(8) Dissenting and/or Concurring Opinions, if any.

To extract these elements from the opinion, it is best to read it several times, going slowly and carefully.

For example, assume that you have read a case concerning a lawsuit between a group of neighbors and a nearby automobile racetrack. The neighbors are unhappy with the noise and traffic generated by the races. How would you go about briefing it?

Case Caption

Start with the case caption. Cite the case in *Bluebook* form, as if the case were going to an appellate court. In general, use parallel cites.

Facts

Describe the parties, not necessarily by name, but by status. Who is the plaintiff and who is the defendant? Here, the plaintiffs are a group of neighbors whose properties abut an automobile racetrack. The defendant is the company that owns the racetrack.

Next, explain what happened to bring the parties to court. Do not use the *Facts* section to describe what happened after the lawsuit was filed. Instead, focus on what happened **before the suit was filed** that caused the plaintiff to sue the defendant and describe it using the past tense. Perhaps the racetrack was built outside of town, but over time development grew up around it. While in the past, the track didn't bother anyone, the increased nearby population now makes its presence problematic. Look at the facts emphasized by the court, particularly those that affected how they analyzed the situation, and summarize them.

Finally, conclude the *Facts* section by identifying the legal basis of the plaintiff's claims against the defendant. This is commonly known as the "cause of action." If the cause of action has several elements, list or describe them. Thus, in your automobile racetrack case, after describing the reason the neighbors are bringing suit against the racetrack, lay out their legal claim against it. Here, assume they are suing under the tort theory known as "nuisance." Describe what a plaintiff must show the court in order to prove that the racetrack is a nuisance and that the neighbors are entitled to some relief.

Depending upon the needs of the person for whom you are writing the case brief, your facts section might range from one to several paragraphs in length.

Example of Facts Section for an Airport Nuisance Case[1]

Facts: Defendant Troutman constructed Carolina Air Park, a private airport, adjacent to the home and medical clinic of Plaintiff Barrier. The end of the airport runway was located 400 yards from Plaintiff's property and approximately 100 feet lower in elevation. When planes landed and took off, they were required to fly low over Plaintiff's property, allegedly disturbing Plaintiff's peace and enjoyment of his home, breaking branches off trees, creating harsh noise, and creating a danger to visitors.

Plaintiff sued Defendants to enjoin the use of the airport on the grounds that it constituted a private nuisance injurious to the Plaintiff. In order to prevail, the plaintiff must show that the airport's location, structure, and manner of use is a private nuisance, and that it is continuous and recurrent, and the injury irreparable.

1. *Barrier v. Troutman*, 231 N.C. 47, 55 S.E.2d 923 (1949).

Procedural History

Here, briefly summarize how the case worked its way through the court system **once it was filed.** Start with trial court's decision: who won at trial? Who appealed? If you are briefing a case at the Supreme Court level, also describe what happened at the Court of Appeals. In whose favor did it rule, and who appealed from that decision? Finish with the appellant's appeal to the court whose decision you are briefing.

Example of Procedural History Section for a Case in the Supreme Court

Procedural History: Plaintiffs sued the Defendant in the Superior Court of Wake County. The trial court ruled in favor of the defendant racetrack. Plaintiffs appealed. The North Carolina Court of Appeals affirmed the trial court's decision. The Supreme Court granted the plaintiff's petition to hear the case.

Issue

The "issue" is a one sentence statement of the question the court is being asked to consider. It should include both the essential facts of the case, and the legal issue at hand so that a person who reads only the issue will know what the case is about and what question of law is before the court. There are different schools of thought on how it should be phrased. Many practitioners prefer that the question begin with the word "whether." Others prefer a more grammatically correct sentence, often starting with the word "does."

Example of the Issue for an Automobile Racetrack Nuisance Case

Whether a neighborhood has a cause of action for nuisance against an automobile racetrack because of the attendant noise, traffic, and pollution, when the neighborhood was developed in close proximity to the racetrack after it had been in operation for a number of years?

or

Does a neighborhood have a cause of action for nuisance against an automobile racetrack because of the attendant noise, traffic and pollution, when the racetrack was developed in close proximity to the neighborhood after it had been in operation for a number of years?

In general, a more detailed statement of the issue is better than a more general one. Consider the following issues for the racetrack case. Which one gives you the most information about the case?

- Whether the plaintiffs have a cause of action?
- Whether the plaintiff neighborhood has a cause of action against the nearby automobile racetrack?
- Whether an automobile racetrack is a nuisance?

- Whether an automobile racetrack in a residential neighborhood is a nuisance?
- Whether an automobile racetrack in a residential neighborhood is a nuisance if the neighborhood was there first?
- Whether an automobile racetrack located near a residential neighborhood which holds races every week for six months of the year, creating noise, traffic and pollution, constitutes a legal nuisance for which a preexisting neighborhood has a cause of action?

As you can see, the more detailed the issue, the more information it conveys. But, you can add so much information that the issue becomes hard to read. Try to reach a balance, conveying the key facts, and the key legal question. However you phrase your issue, make it in the form of a question that can be answered "yes" or "no."

Holding

In this section of the case brief, state the court's decision in the case, i.e., its answer to the question posed in the issue. Customs vary on how to state the holding: some prefer that you simply write, "yes," or "no." Others prefer that you restate the issue in the form of a statement that answers the question:

Example of a Holding in the Negative

A neighborhood does not have a cause of action for nuisance against an automobile racetrack because of the attendant noise, traffic, and pollution, when the neighborhood was developed in close proximity to the racetrack after it had been in operation for a number of years.

A well written holding conveys the essential facts of the case, the legal question at issue, and the court's answer to it, such that the reader does not have to look at any other section of the brief. The holding in the example mirrors the words of the issue as originally phrased above. The primary difference is that the word "not" was inserted to answer the question in the negative. If the answer were in the affirmative, the holding could be stated as follows.

Example of a Holding in the Affirmative

A neighborhood has a cause of action for nuisance against an automobile racetrack because of the attendant noise, traffic and pollution, when the neighborhood was developed in close proximity to the racetrack after it had been in operation for a number of years.

Rationale/Reasoning

In the "Rationale" or "Reasoning" section of the brief, explain the basis for the court's decision. Why did the court rule in favor of the plaintiffs or defendants? Courts typically base their decisions on one or more of the following factors:

1. precedent
2. statutory construction
3. legislative intent
4. public policy.

Precedent is a previously decided case similar to the one before the court on which the court relies to make a decision. Often, the same kinds of facts and issues will come before a court again and again. The first time the court considers such a case, it may establish a rule of law for how such cases should be decided in the future. The court can then return to its previous decisions for direction on how to handle current disputes.

The adherence of the court to its prior decisions is known as the doctrine of *stare decisis*, a Latin term which means to "abide by" or "adhere to" decided cases. The doctrine of *stare decisis* requires a court to adhere to precedent; that is, to follow its own decisions and decisions of higher courts in its jurisdiction.

What is the purpose of a rule requiring a court to adhere to earlier decisions? Consistency and fairness. The theory behind the doctrine of *stare decisis* is that if, the court consistently follows precedents, society will be guided in how to act and parties in similar situations will be treated similarly.

Of course, society is constantly changing, and so the doctrine of *stare decisis* is not absolute. Consider a well known example—the case of Plessy v. Ferguson, 163 U.S. 537 (1896). In this case, the United States Supreme Court held that "separate but equal" treatment of persons of color does not violate the United States Constitution. Then, over fifty years later, the United States Supreme Court considered the case of Brown v. Board of Education, 347 U.S. 483 (1954). Had it followed the doctrine of *stare decisis* and adhered to precedent, the Court might have ruled that separate but equal school systems are constitutional. Instead, the Court held that when such schools are separate, they are inherently unequal and therefore unconstitutional. The Court explicitly overturned Plessy v. Ferguson, saying that it had been wrong. Thus, the United States Supreme Court ignored its own precedent in this case.

Statutory construction is the process of interpreting any applicable statute. Although legislatures generally attempt to draft statutes that are clear, sometimes the application of a law to a particular factual situation is not obvious. Courts routinely analyze the language of the law and apply it to particular disputes.

Closely aligned with the exercise of statutory construction is the determination of **legislative intent**. When a statute is ambiguous, or its application to a particular fact situation unclear, a court may try to determine the intent of the legislature in adopting the statute in the first place. What policy was the legislature trying to advance? What wrong was it trying to correct? In this way, the court may be guided in applying the law to the suit at hand.

Finally, courts are guided in their decisions by **public policy**, that is, general principles of what is best for the welfare of the citizens of the state.

Judgment

In this section of your case brief, concisely state the ultimate decision of the appellate court whose case you are briefing. For example, if the appellate court agrees with the decision of the court below, then your judgment section could simply say, "affirmed." Or, if the court disagrees with the decision of the court below, the judgment section should say, "reversed." Sometimes the court agrees with parts of the lower courts ruling but disagrees with others. In such cases, the judgment is "affirmed in part, reversed in part." Often, the court's decision involves sending the case back to the trial court to do something over ("remand"), in which case, this too will be part of the judgment. In most written opinions, the judgment is easy to find, and is often the last sentence of the majority's opinion.

Dissenting and Concurring Opinions

Appellate court decisions in North Carolina are decided by more than one judge. Those of the Court of Appeals are typically decided by three-judge panels. Cases before the North Carolina Supreme Court are often decided by all seven justices sitting together as a panel. Of course, members of the appellate courts do not always agree with each other. When the opinion of the judges or justices hearing an appeal is not unanimous, those in the majority write the opinion for the court. If a judge agrees with the majority's decision but for different reasons, the judge may write a concurring opinion. Similarly, one or more judges in the minority may choose to write a "dissenting opinion" where they take issue with the majority's decision and explain why they believe the case should have been decided another way.

Sample Brief

Jones v. Queen City Speedways, Inc., 276 N.C. 231, 172 S.E.2d 42 (1970).

Facts: Defendant Speedway constructed and operated a racetrack in a light industrial district across the street from the residential district where plaintiffs resided. The noise of the racetrack was so loud that it was annoying to the plaintiffs, caused them to lose sleep at night, and impaired their use and enjoyment of their homes. In addition, the value of the plaintiffs' property depreciated because of the noise, light, and dust generated by the track, and made their homes virtually uninhabitable while races were in progress.

Plaintiffs sought an injunction barring the operation of the track based upon the doctrine of "nuisance" and pursuant to prohibitions in a local ordinance against noise. In order to demonstrate they are entitled to injunctive relief based upon the theory of nuisance, plaintiffs must show that the noise was unreasonable for normal people given its location, time, frequency, and effect. In order to violate the ordinance (No. 62), the track must generate regularly recurring noise that exceeds the normal noise level generated by uses permitted in residential and office districts.

Procedural History: Plaintiffs sued to enjoin the operation of the racetrack owned by Defendant. The jury found that the Defendant located, used and operated its track so as to constitute a nuisance. The trial judge ordered various corrective measures by the Defendants to reduce the noise, dust and glare. Plaintiffs' petition to the North Carolina Supreme Court for certiorari was granted; the Court agreed to hear the case before determination by the Court of Appeals.

Issue: Whether the operation of a racetrack adjacent to a residential neighborhood must be enjoined when a jury finds that the track is a nuisance because it generates a great level of noise in excess of that which is customary in residential districts, to the detriment of the residential property owners.

Holding: Yes. The operation of a racetrack adjacent to a residential neighborhood must be enjoined when a jury finds that the track is a nuisance because it generates a great level of noise in excess of that which is customary in residential districts to the detriment of the residential property owners.

Rationale: The operation of a racetrack is a lawful enterprise, and therefore is not a nuisance per se. However, circumstances can result in it being a private nuisance *per accidens*. *Hooks v. Int'l Speedways, Inc.*, 263 N.C. 686, 140 S.E.2d 387 (1965). Factors include the location, intensity, disagreeableness of the sounds, time, frequency, and effect on normal, reasonable people. *Id.*

Further, local ordinance prohibits in this area of the city regularly recurring noises that exceed the normal noise level generated by uses permitted in residential and office districts. Although violation of the ordinance does not necessarily constitute a nuisance, if the track activity is a nuisance and it violates a municipal ordinance, relief may be obtained by someone who suffers special and peculiar injury as a result.

Courts in similar cases have found the noise generated by airports and racetracks is a nuisance and that the only possible remedy is to completely restrain the activity. Although a court will not outlaw an entire operation if restrictions on its operation will eliminate the injury, the trial court was not authorized to supervise a track's operation. *Hooks, supra.* Even if it could, the trial court's order allowed even more activity than the jury already ruled was a nuisance. Plaintiffs were therefore entitled to a judgment restraining the track's operation.

Judgment: Error and remanded for entry of a judgment on the verdict restraining the alleged nuisance.

Exercise 7 — Case Brief

Write a case brief for the 1970 case appearing in volume 7 of the *North Carolina Court of Appeals Reports* on page 463, and also appearing in the S.E.2d, involving a suit by the Deacons of the Sandy Branch Baptist Church against a hog packing company.

Chapter 8

Administrative Law

Administrative law is created by administrative agencies, and includes rules and case opinions. It is another source of primary authority.

Most administrative agencies are part of the executive branch of government and are subject to the ultimate authority of the chief executive: the president of the United States or the governor of the State of North Carolina, for example.

The traditional function of the executive branch of government is to "execute" or administer laws created by the legislative branch, that is, to put them into effect. This cannot be done by the legislature or executive officer alone. Very often, it requires action by persons with greater expertise. Agencies are designed to fill that role.

Consider the following federal agencies: the Federal Aviation Administration, Environmental Protection Agency, Nuclear Regulatory Commission, Federal Trade Commission, Food & Drug Administration, Interstate Commerce Commission, Securities & Exchange Commission, National Labor Relations Board, Social Security Administration, and of course the Internal Revenue Service. These agencies govern a myriad of topics, some of which can be quite complex. They have a pervasive impact on your daily life, from airplane safety, to automobile emission standards, to nutrition labels on prepackaged foods.

North Carolina has a large number of state agencies as well. Some mirror the functions of federal agencies, like the Division of Environment and Natural Resources. Others are found only in State government, for example the various occupational licensing boards that oversee the licensed professions. Other state agencies include the North Carolina Secretary of State (which oversees corporations and other businesses, notaries, and the sale of securities), the Department of Insurance, and the Department of Labor.

The role of government agencies has increased with the complexity of modern society. A hundred years ago, the legislative branch may have had the necessary expertise to deal with most of the issues facing the nation. Today, those issues often require the input of specialists who understand the technology or intricacies that are included in the area of law at hand. For example, most legislators know little about pollution controlling devices on automobiles. Legislators can express a policy that air pollution be reduced, but experts are needed to craft rules outlining how it should be done, and to make determinations about whether violations of the law have occurred. Thus, agencies are filled with experts in the field they regulate.

Enabling Statutes

Although most administrative agencies are part of the executive branch of government, agencies are first created by the legislative branch. When the legislature determines that it needs to delegate certain of its powers to a body with the expertise necessary to regulate a particular subject area or group of people, it adopts a law called an "enabling statute." The enabling statute creates the agency and gives it the authority to regulate.

For example, in 1933 the legislature adopted enabling legislation to create the North Carolina State Bar. The Bar was given the authority to regulate the practice of law by attorneys. See N.C. Gen. Stat. §§ 84-15 to -88 (2003). The enabling legislation is still in effect today, and outlines the purpose of the Bar, its ruling council, and its authority to adopt rules. Under this authority, the Bar then creates the rules regulating the conduct of lawyers, and also takes action against lawyers as necessary to enforce its rules.

---

§ 84-15. Creation of North Carolina State Bar as an agency of the State.

There is hereby created as an agency of the State of North Carolina, for the purposes and with the powers hereinafter set forth, the North Carolina State Bar. (1933, s. 1.)

Enabling statutes typically confer on the agency a variety of powers, including a quasi-legislative function, a quasi-judicial function, and an enforcement function. Thus, in some ways, an agency is like all three branches of government in one!

Quasi-Legislative Function

Agencies have the power to create law, in the form of rules or regulations. (The terms "rules" and "regulations" are generally interchangeable.) Rules and regulations must be obeyed by the people and/or companies regulated by the agency, but not by anyone else. Thus, they are said to apply only to a "regulated class" of people.

For example, the North Carolina Commission for Health Services is required by statute to adopt and enforce drinking water rules to regulate the public water systems. N.C. Gen. Stat. § 130A-315 (2003). The rules specify the maximum contaminant levels, treatment techniques, and procedures to assure an adequate water supply.

Enforcement Function

The enabling statutes that create agencies give those agencies the power to enforce their rules. Included in that power is the right to investigate violations, file administrative actions or suits to enforce the law, and act as prosecutor of those who violate the rules. Thus, if the Commission for Health Services finds that its drinking water rules are not being carried out, it can take enforcement action against the violator.

Quasi-Judicial Function

Agencies also function as a court and hear cases where violations of their rules are alleged. They may also hear cases involving disputes between the agency and the public.

The case of *Clark Stone Co. v. N.C. Division of Environment & Natural Resources*, 164 N.C. App. 24, 594 S.E.2d 832 (2004) illustrates the powers of many agencies, and how their judicial function works. The case revolved around a mining *permit* issued by the Division of Environment and Natural Resources ("DENR"). Permitting is a common function of agencies. DENR revoked the permit after determining that it had been issued on insufficient information, and violated the Mining Act. Clark Stone Company brought a "contested case proceeding" before DENR, arguing that the permit should not have been revoked. DENR made the ultimate decision in the case, determining its revocation of the permit was proper. In hearing the contested case and making its decision, DENR was performing a judicial function. Its written opinion in the case is law, and is primary authority.

Agency Judges

The judges who hear administrative agency cases vary, depending upon the agency. For instance, some administrative agencies hear their own cases. When they do, the decision may be made by the appointed members of the agency or by an agency official. However, most agency cases are heard not by the agency itself, but a separate and impartial Administrative Law Judge ("ALJ"). The ALJ's decision is typically appealable back to the agency itself.

In North Carolina, most agencies bring their cases before ALJs at a separate state agency known as the "Office of Administrative Hearings" or "OAH." This office was established by the legislature to assure that agency decisions are made in a fair and impartial manner. By separating the decision-making from the agency involved, the apparent conflict of interest which otherwise exists is minimized.

A few North Carolina agencies still hear their own cases. These agencies are delineated in the General Statutes, Chapter 150B, Article 3A. They include occupational licensing agencies, certain banking and insurance agencies, and the State Building Code Council.

Administrative Hearings and Agency Decisions

Administrative hearings are much like a trial in civil or criminal court. The Rules of Evidence generally apply, although sometimes more loosely than in court. Witnesses testify under oath and are cross-examined, evidence is received, and a decision rendered.

Agency decisions are written much like the decisions of a court. However, most are not collected and published in reporters. This makes them hard to research, unless they are appealed to a court whose decisions are reported.

Protection from Agency Abuses

Agencies are unique in that their functions are unified: they can be a legislature, prosecutor, judge and jury, all in one. In an effort to put experts in charge of the rule-making and judicial process for areas requiring special knowledge, agencies have been given the power to makes their own rules, try cases against perceived violators, and decide whether a violation has in fact occurred. This combination of functions has resulted in criticism that agencies wield too much power.

To protect the regulated classes from abuse of power by administrative agencies, Congress adopted the federal Administrative Procedure Act ("APA")[1] in 1946. Similarly, North Carolina adopted its own Administrative Procedures Act (also known as the "APA")[2] in 1973. Both the federal and state APAs place restraints on the agencies' legislative and judicial functions.

Both the federal and state APAs mandate **procedures** an agency must follow to create and enforce its rules. Rule-making requires notice of proposed rules to those affected and opportunity for public comment. Hearings include the right to present evidence, cross-examine witnesses, and other requirements of due process. Many agencies are required to bring their cases before an independent Administrative Law Judge. And, adverse agency decisions are appealable to the state or federal courts.

---

1. 5 U.S.C. §§ 551 to 559, 701 to 706, 1305, 3105, 4301, 5335, 5372, 7521 (2000)
2. N.C. Gen. Stat. § 150B-1 to -52 (2003)

Research in Rules/Regulations

Suppose that you need to find out a particular agency rule or regulation. For example, perhaps you need to find out what the EPA or DENR regulations are regarding water run-off from paved surfaces or asbestos in public buildings. Or, maybe your client wants to "go public" and offer shares of stock to investors? Or, perhaps your client simply wants to incorporate. Where do you go to find administrative law?

Federal Rules/Regulations

There are two main publications of federal agency actions and rules: the *Federal Register* and the *Code of Federal Regulations ("C.F.R.")*.

The Federal Register

The *Federal Register* is a publication created by an Act of Congress: the "Federal Register Act" of 1935. The *Federal Register* is a daily publication that looks much like a tabloid newspaper (but with fewer pictures). It contains reports on all the federal administrative and executive actions.

The federal APA requires that certain items be included in the *Federal Register*:

- notice of proposed rule-making;
- notice of any public hearing on proposed rules;
- the text of proposed federal agency rules/regulations; and
- the text of new federal agency rules/regulations.

No regulation is valid unless it is adopted in accordance with this process.

The Code of Federal Regulations (C.F.R.)

The *C.F.R.* also was created by Congress in an amendment to the Federal Register Act. The *C.F.R.* is a compilation of federal agency regulations arranged by subject matter. Much like the U.S. Code, the *C.F.R.* has fifty titles on similar topics. Within each title are "Parts" that are equivalent in some ways to chapters. Within each part are individual sections.

The *C.F.R.* is revised annually, one volume at a time. Each year, the volumes are printed in a new color. Thus, when you look at the *C.F.R.* on the shelf, you will note that some volumes are one color, and the rest another. Because they are not updated in order, the two colors will be mixed together. You can tell at a glance which ones have been recently updated, and which are older.

Finding Federal Administrative Rules/Regulations

Generally, you will begin your research into federal administrative law questions by looking for the enabling statute. It will give you an overview of the agency involved, its authority, and the subject matter it regulates. When you find an enabling statute, you will often find a cross-reference in the U.S.C., the U.S.C.A., and the U.S.C.S. to at least some of the applicable *C.F.R.* sections.

If you prefer, you can skip the enabling statute and search directly in the *C.F.R.* It has a subject matter index—a hard-bound series of books called the *Index to the Code of Federal Regulations*, and also a soft-bound index called the *Index and Finding Aids Volume*, which is generally the easiest to find and use.

Practice Set 8.1

Suppose you are researching a question concerning fair housing.

Look up the Fair Housing Act in the U.S. Code's subject matter index or Popular Names Table. You will find a reference to 42 U.S.C. §§ 36001–3619. Within the notes on these sections are cross-references to the *C.F.R.*, Title 24, Part 100. Find them.

Next, look up "Fair Housing" in the indexes to the *C.F.R.* Find the references to Title 24 of the *C.F.R.*, Parts 100 and following.

Citing Federal Rules/Regulations

The Bluebook's Rule 14.2 covers the most commonly cited administrative materials. It requires you to cite any administrative rule or regulation to the *C.F.R.* if possible. The citation includes, at a minimum,

- the applicable *C.F.R.* title number,
- the abbreviation, "C.F.R.,"
- either the section symbol ("§") and number of the particular section cited, or the abbreviation, "Pt." for "Part" and the number of the larger part cited, and
- the year of the code edition, in parentheses, at the end of the cite.

Examples of citations to the *C.F.R.*

24 C.F.R. pt. 100 (2005)

24 C.F.R. § 100.50 (2005)

Give the name of the rule or regulation only if it is commonly known by that name. The example in *The Bluebook*, updated to a more current version, is:

FTC Credit Practices Rules, 16 C.F.R. pt. 444 (2005).

Giving a rule name is rarely necessary. Thus, a specific rule may be cited as either:

FTC Credit Practices Rule, 16 C.F.R. § 444.2 (2005).

or

16 C.F.R. § 444.2 (2005)

In the preceding three citations, "16" is the title number of the *Code of Federal Regulations*. In the first one, "pt. 444" is the part containing all the sections on FTC Credit Practices. In the other two citations, "§ 444.2" is a particular section within part 444. The year, "(2005)," is the year of the latest volume of the *C.F.R.* in which the rule can be found.

As required by *Bluebook* Rule 14.2, cite to the most recent edition (unless you are citing an older version for historical purposes). In order to assure that you have the most current version of a rule, check the date on the *C.F.R.* volume. It should be either the year it is now, or the previous year.

Even if the volume appears to be up-to-date, make sure that you have the most current version of the section or part of the Code you are citing. Do this by checking a monthly supplement for the *C.F.R.* called the *List of C.F.R. Sections Affected* (*"LSA"*). If the sections you are researching have been amended, they will be listed in the *LSA*, along with a reference to a page number in the *Federal Register*. You must then go to that page in the *Register* to see the actual changes to the rule.

If you cannot find the *LSA*, you can go directly to the *Federal Register* to check for amendments. At the back of each issue, in the "Readers Aids" section, is a list of *C.F.R.* parts affected during that month. Look at the latest issue for each month since the *C.F.R.* was printed. There, you will find a list of any part of the *C.F.R.* affected by recent amendments, and a reference to the page in the *Federal Register* where the change appears.

North Carolina Rules/Regulations

The North Carolina APA requires that state agencies publish notices of proposed rules, scheduled rule-making hearings, and the text of adopted rules, in a publication called the **North Carolina Register**. It is akin to the *Federal Register* but covers only North Carolina rules. It is published approximately every two weeks. It is also available online at Office of Administrative Hearings (OAH) web-site: http://www.oah.state.nc.us/rules/register/.

North Carolina state agency rules are set out in the **North Carolina Administrative Code** ("NCAC" or "N.C. Admin. Code"). The North Carolina Administrative Code includes 28 titles and is organized by subject matter. West publishes the North Carolina Administrative Code in a dark blue, softbound set, updated monthly. It also is available on disk, and through subscriber-based computer research services like *Lexis* and *Westlaw*. And, it is available online at http://ncrules.state.nc.us/ncad ministrativ_/default.htm or via the OAH web-site: www.oah.state.nc.us.

If you cannot access the rules you need through any of the above sources, contact the agency in question directly. Most agencies publish their rules in paper form, and on the agency's website.

Citing North Carolina Administrative Rules/Regulations

To cite a North Carolina administrative rule or regulation in accordance with *The Bluebook*, use table T.1. Go to the North Carolina section of T.1 and look under the bold heading, "**Administrative compilation.**" *The Bluebook* will confirm there that North Carolina's administrative compilation is called the "North Carolina Administrative Code," and that it is cited:

x N.C. Admin. Code x.x (year)

The first "x" is for the title number, and the series, "x.x" represents the rule number, which will in fact include a period in the middle. The year is the date of publication of the code book. For example,

8 N.C. Admin. Code 04.0301 (2002)

(Citation modified in accordance with the *Bluepages*.)

However, you will note that the NC Administrative Code abbreviates itself differently than is called for in *The Bluebook*. Many agencies prefer that you adopt the Code's standard for abbreviation, namely, x NCAC x.x. For example,

8 NCAC 04 .0301 (or 08 NCAC 04. 0301).

If an agency or other tribunal expresses a preference for a particular form of citation, always follow the expressly preferred method.

Exercise 8 — Administrative Law

1. Look up the Equal Employment Opportunity Commission in the U.S.C.A.

    A. Cite the statute creating the Commission.

    B. Search the notes, annotations, and references following the statute cited above for a cross-reference to the EEOC in the C.F.R. Cite in *Bluebook* form the part or section referenced.

    C. What is the referenced part about?

    D. Cite the part of the C.F.R. that has been reprinted in the U.S.C.A.

    E. What are the sections in "Subpart B" about?

    F. Where does an aggrieved person make a charge? (Answer the question and cite the pertinent section.)

2. Find 42 U.S.C.A. § 2021c (West 2003) concerning the responsibility for disposal of low-level radioactive waste.

    A. Go to the first section listed in the C.F.R. and cite it in *Bluebook* form.

    B. Which agency's rules are these?

    C. Where do the rules of that agency begin? Cite the first section. (For assistance, look at the page at the front of the volume titled, "THIS TITLE.")

    D. What is the first section about?

    E. Cite the first section of the cross-referenced *enabling statute*. (*Bluebook* form is not required.)

3. Look up "Privacy" in the softbound C.F.R. Index, and within that topic, "Homeland Security Department."

    A. What sub-topic and section are listed? (*Bluebook* form not required.)

    B.   Look up that part in the C.F.R. and list the three subparts of the rules.

4.   Look up the North Carolina State Bar's rules on the OAH website.

    A.   The Bar's rules are in which title?

    B.   Go to chapter 1, Subchapter B of the Bar's rules. Find the rule describing the "Procedure for Professional Discipline." Cite it twice, first as it appears on the website, and second in *Bluebook* form. Omit the volume date since you are not using one.

Chapter 9

Secondary Authority

Secondary authorities are legal research materials that are not themselves the law, but that talk about the law, analyze or describe it. These resources are most helpful when you know little about the area you have been assigned to research, and need some background information. Secondary authorities can give you a succinct summary of the law on a given topic and help you focus your understanding of the issues. This will allow you to conduct your research more efficiently.

Remember, however, that secondary authorities are at best persuasive to a court, depending upon the source. They are never mandatory authority; that is, a court is not required to follow the law as described by a secondary authority.

Secondary authorities often serve as *de facto* finding tools for primary and other secondary authorities, both on the particular topic they address, and on related topics. Thus, you can use secondary authorities as a "jumping off" point for your research. If you find a good one, a large part of your preliminary research will have been done for you.

The type of secondary authority you choose depends on how much you know about the topic, and the depth of detail you are seeking. For example, **dictionaries** and **encyclopedias** provide definitions of key terms and a broad overview of the law. **Treatises, hornbooks** and even law school **study aids** can provide a more detailed level of discussion, but are still general enough to help you understand the area of law you are researching in relatively straightforward terms. However, many of these books focus on the law on a national, rather than state, level. Depending upon the topic, you may find books on state law too.

For in-depth analysis, secondary authorities like *American Law Reports* ("A.L.R.") and periodicals can give you more details on particular questions. Law review and journal articles are periodicals that provide an academic approach, typically at a high level of scholarship, on current or controversial issues. They may include the author's opinion about what the law should be. And, many address issues that are state-specific.

If you are looking for a resource that attempts to include everything you can think of on a particular subject, including both primary and secondary authority, and also finding tools, look to a **loose-leaf** service.

Legal Dictionaries

The legal vocabulary can be difficult for anyone new to the field. Even experienced legal professionals come upon unknown words or phrases from time to time. To help you understand the authorities you read, whenever you embark on a new research project, it is wise to have a legal dictionary at your side. Some will merely define the legal terms you come across in your research, from the ancient to the modern and technical. Others attempt to go farther, giving excerpts from cases, complete with citations, and overviews of changes or trends in the law.

Most dictionaries define words and concepts that occur in court opinions, statutes, regulations and other legal documents. While *Black's Law Dictionary* and *Ballentine's* are perhaps the best known, there are many others. In many law libraries, you will find a dictionary on every table. In addition, online legal dictionaries now proliferate, giving you definitions for legal words and phrases for free, wherever you are (so long as you have internet access). You should make a practice of looking up all unknown terms as you go. Learning their meaning will help you refine your understanding of the law and will ultimately speed your research.

Reprinted with the permission of West, a Thomson Business.

Citing a Legal Dictionary

Rarely will you cite a dictionary. Although you will use them regularly to help you understand the law, dictionaries are secondary authority on the most fundamental level, and are not typically persuasive authorities on a point of law. It is not often that you have to convince the court of the definition of a particular word.

Should you ever need to cite a dictionary, use *The Bluebook's* Rule 15.8 on special citation forms. (See also the *Bluepages* at B8.1.) This Rule covers both dictionaries and encyclopedias, and directs you by example. Accordingly, cite dictionaries by their name, followed by the page number on which the word or phrase you are citing is found, with no comma in between. Put a parenthetical at the end of your citation containing the edition of the dictionary you used, and the date of that edition.

Remember to convert your citation to ordinary roman type, rather than using all capital letters pursuant to *The Bluebook's* Rule P. 1 in the *Practitioners' Notes*. And, underline or italicize the dictionary name.

Sample Citations to a Dictionary

Black's Law Dictionary 485 (5th ed. 2004)

Black's Law Dictionary 485 (5th ed. 2004)

Words and Phrases

Words and Phrases is a set of books, published by Thomson West, that works like an expanded legal dictionary. It provides definitions of words and phrases as set down in court opinions. It is like a dictionary in that it is in alphabetical order and doesn't require a separate index. However, the words and phrases are summarized in more detail—so much so that it takes about 50 volumes to get from A to Z. Many of the words included are defined generally, and then in various different contexts, including citations to cases that addressed them. Thus, it may take several pages to get through the discussion about one word or phrase. As always, don't forget to check the supplement—there is an annual cumulative pocket part that adds more case summaries for the words and phrases you are researching, from the date of the main volume forward.

Encyclopedias

Encyclopedias summarize almost every area of the law. They are organized by subject matter in alphabetical order. In general, the summaries start with a short and objective statement of the law on the topic at hand. These statements are often in bold type, and are known as "black letter" law. They are followed by a more detailed explanation with footnotes cross-referencing the reader to cases on point. Even so, encyclopedias are general references, and will not provide you with a high degree of analysis of any particular point. They will give you a good summary of the law, and are useful as background information.

There are two main national encyclopedias: *Corpus Juris Secundum*, ("C.J.S.") and *American Jurisprudence* ("Am. Jur."). C.J.S. is dark blue; its 160+ volumes occupy several shelves in any library. Am. Jur. is dark green. While slightly smaller, it still takes up about 140 volumes on the shelf.

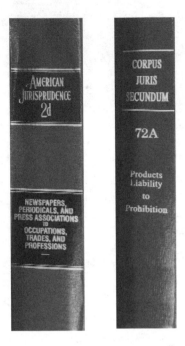

"Reprinted with the permission of West, a Thomson Business."

Both C.J.S. and Am. Jur. divide the law into more than 400 major subject areas. Historically, C.J.S. has attempted to be more comprehensive. (*Corpus Juris means, literally, "the body of the law."*) In contrast, Am. Jur. has chosen a smaller representative sample of pertinent cases. Both sets emphasize case law over statutes. Because C.J.S. and Am. Jur. are now both published by West, each provides cross-references to other West products using the key number system. Whether you choose one set or the other is largely a matter of personal preference. In general, you need not look at both, as their coverage will overlap. However, if you are having trouble finding a particular point of law in one set, try the other. Your indexing words may yield better results in one set versus the other because the editors who decide on the indexing words are different. Look at Figure 9.1 for a sample page from C.J.S.

There are also some state-specific encyclopedias. For example, some would consider *Strong's North Carolina Index* an encyclopedia. However, because it also functions as a digest, it was addressed previously in Chapter 5. *Strong's* summarizes North Carolina case law, statutes, and court rules. It is organized topically and consists of more than forty volumes. It has separate index volumes to aid your search for information and authorities on its topics.

reasonably anticipated.[3] Where the appliance is not inherently or imminently dangerous, there is no such liability,[4] unless the defendant had knowledge of the defective nature of the appliance.[5]

Where a household appliance explodes or ignites while being used for its intended purpose, resulting in injury to its ultimate consumer or user, the liability of the manufacturer may be established based on a theory of a design defect that renders the product inherently dangerous.[6] The duty to warn theory does not apply in circumstances where a defect in the design of a product renders it dangerous per se to use as intended.[7]

§ 96   Household appliances—
Liability of retailer

Although a retailer of household appliances is generally not liable for defects of which it was unaware, it is liable where it holds itself out as the manufacturer of the

appliance.

Research References

West's Key Number Digest, Products Liability ⊜52

Strict liability does not apply to a nonmanufacturing importer or retailer,[1] especially for design defects.[2] The liability of the retailer is limited to the contract.[3]

However, in the marketing of its products the retailer might undertake and assume a special responsibility toward the members of the consuming public who might be injured by a defect in the product, including persons who were not parties to the initial sale by the

---

[3]Ill.—Beadles v. Servel Inc., 344 Ill. App. 133, 100 N.E.2d 405 (3d Dist. 1951).

[4]U.S.—Borg-Warner Corporation (Norge Division) v. Heine, 128 F.2d 657 (C.C.A. 6th Cir. 1942).

Ohio—Blissenbach v. Yanko, 90 Ohio App. 557, 48 Ohio Op. 203, 107 N.E.2d 409 (7th Dist. Mahoning County 1951).

Body vibrating machine

Ga.—Robbins v. Georgia Power Co., 47 Ga. App. 517, 171 S.E. 218 (1933).

Exercising device

N.Y.—Heggblom v. John Wanamaker, New York, 178 Misc. 792, 36 N.Y.S.2d 777 (Sup 1942).

[5]Mass.—McCabe v. Boston Consol. Gas Co., 314 Mass. 493, 50 N.E.2d 640 (1943).

[6]**Refrigerator**

N.C.—Fowler v. General Elec. Co., 40 N.C. App. 301, 252 S.E.2d 862, 26 U.C.C. Rep. Serv. 350 (1979).

[7]**Expert testimony**

There was expert testimony that the safety thermostat on a refrigerator icemaker was not designed to cut off the power automatically and, thus, the heater that warmed the mold so as to release ice cubes into the storage pan raised the heat to the point where it melted the insulation on the wiring, which then caused the wiring to fuse and arc, resulting in a fire; although the icemaker was not an inherently dangerous product, the only step which the consumer could have taken to avoid dangers from the use of the icemaker would have been to not use the machine at all.

N.C.—Fowler v. General Elec. Co., 40 N.C. App. 301, 252 S.E.2d 862, 26 U.C.C. Rep. Serv. 350 (1979).

[Section 96]
[1]**Appliance received in original box**

The user of a fondue pot, who had received it as a gift in its original unbroken carton from its purchaser, and who was injured when the pot spun over on its handle and spilled hot cooking oil on her leg, could not maintain an action based on strict liability against the pot's importer or retailer, or the company which was apparently the retailer's parent company, because none were the manufacturer of the pot.

Ga.—Ellis v. Rich's, Inc., 233 Ga. 573, 212 S.E.2d 373, 16 U.C.C. Rep. Serv. 683 (1975).

[2]**Dishwasher**

The vendor of a dishwasher could not be liable on strict liability or negligent design and manufacturing defect claims brought by a consumer who bought the dishwasher, the door of which allegedly posed a tripping hazard, where the vendor did not design or manufacture the dishwasher.

U.S.—Levine v. Sears Roebuck and Co., 200 F. Supp. 2d 180 (E.D. N.Y. 2002) (applying New York law).

[3]**Sale with maintenance contract**

A transaction in which a consumer purchased a dishwasher from a vendor and in which the vendor contracted to repair the dishwasher was not a hybrid service-sale transaction which would give rise to a cause of action for breach of warranty or strict liability, where the consumer bought the dishwasher almost 17 years before the underlying alleged accident, entered into a separate maintenance agreement with the vendor, and renewed the maintenance agreement every two years.

U.S.—Levine v. Sears Roebuck and Co., 200 F. Supp. 2d 180 (E.D. N.Y. 2002) (applying New York law).

146

Figure 9.1   Reprinted with the permission of West, a Thomson Business.

Use an encyclopedia as a starting point when you need background information on a particular topic. Encyclopedias contain a relatively objective and straightforward overview, and their general statements of the law are easy to understand.

You can also use encyclopedias as a finding tool for relevant cases on the topic and as an entry into West's key number system. In addition, Am. Jur. is an excellent source for A.L.R. articles (see below). Case references are set out in footnotes. Find the point of law relevant to your research topic, and then scan the footnotes for any cases on that point. Each footnote will clearly identify the state from which the case originated. If you are interested in only North Carolina cases, you may decide to start your search with *Strong's*.

Using an Encyclopedia

To use any encyclopedia, start with its "General Index" volumes. These are located at the end of the set, and are typically softbound. Develop a list of indexing words on your topic and use them to get to the right spot in the encyclopedia.

As you read each encyclopedia entry, you will notice that every point is followed by a footnote number. The footnotes are printed on the bottom half of the page, and refer to cases from across the jurisdiction covered by the encyclopedia (the entire country for C.J.S. and Am. Jur.; North Carolina for *Strong's*). There are occasional references to statutes and rules. You can easily scan the footnotes in a national encyclopedia for cases and authorities from North Carolina, or any other state in which you are interested.

Citing an Encyclopedia

Like dictionaries, encyclopedias are secondary authority, and are not especially persuasive to a court. You should therefore avoid citing them unless you have nothing better. However, encyclopedias are at least more detailed than a dictionary, and can be useful for demonstrating the wide acceptance of a particular legal point. Thus, from time to time, it is necessary to cite an entry from an encyclopedia.

There is no separate *Bluebook* rule for citation of encyclopedias. Instead, their citation is covered by Rule 15.8 on "Special Citation Forms" (the same rule that covers citation of dictionaries.) Again, the rule teaches only by example—one for C.J.S. and one for Am. Jur.

The example in *The Bluebook* for C.J.S. is: "88 C.J.S. *Trial* § 192 (1955)." Here, the number "88" is the volume number, found on the spine of the book. "C.J.S." with no spaces, and three periods, is the appropriate abbreviation for the full name of the encyclopedia: "*Corpus Juris Secundum.*" The word "*Trial,*" is the name of the overriding topic or article in which the section you are citing is found. Section ("§") 192 is the specific section being cited within the topic of "*Trial.*"

A common mistake in citing encyclopedias is to use the name or title of the particular section being cited in the citation. Instead, be certain to use the full subject matter article or topic in which the particular section is found. The full name of the article appears at its beginning, just ahead of section one. The article name, or a shortened version of it, also can be found at the top of each page (the "header"). Technically, you should use the full name of the article (as it appears at the beginning), rather than a shortened version that appears at the top of each page.

For example, look at the sample C.J.S. page printed in Figure 9.1. The overriding topic is "PRODUCTS LIABILITY," but it is not shown because it is on the facing page. Section 96 is about "Household Appliances—Liability of Retailer." The proper citation of section 96 is set out below.

Sample Citation to C.J.S.

72A C.J.S. <u>Products Liability</u> § 96 (2004)

or

72A C.J.S. *Products Liability* § 96 (2004).

Note that the underlined or italicized title is "Products Liability," not "Household Appliances—Liability of the Retailer."

The citation of C.J.S. requires no conversion from the format cited in *The Bluebook*. Citing C.J.S. is exactly the same for practitioners as for law review writers. If you choose, you can use underlining instead of italics: "88 C.J.S. <u>Trial</u> § 192 (1955)" and "88 C.J.S. *Trial* § 192 (1955)" are both correct.

The *Bluebook* example for Am. Jur. is: "17 Am. Jur. 2d *Contracts* § 74 (1964)." Here, the abbreviated name of the encyclopedia must be converted to ordinary roman type, as follows.

Sample Citation to Am. Jur.

17 Am. Jur. 2d <u>Contracts</u> § 74 (1964)

17 Am. Jur. 2d *Contracts* § 74 (1964).

Again, you may underline or use italics for the name of the section:

Treatises

A "treatise" is a book written by an expert or scholar on a particular legal topic. It may be one volume or many, softbound, hardbound or even a loose-leaf. If all you need is general background information, then an encyclopedia will do the job. But if you need a detailed analysis of a particular topic, a treatise may be more useful. There are both state-specific and national treatises available.

Most treatises have both an index at the end, and a table of contents up front to help you find the specific information you need. They may also have tables of authorities, such as statutes and cases. Treatises are typically divided into chapters, and within each chapter, into numbered sections or paragraphs. Often, the sections or paragraphs include a heading or topic in bold, to help you narrow your search. The text in each section is typically footnoted. Look to the footnotes at the bottom of the page to find cases and other authorities that support the ideas described in the text.

As you read the narrative in a treatise, you may notice that the author has an express point of view. For example, the author may criticize a particular line of cases, or express an opinion on how the law should be interpreted in a particular area. Thus, treatises can help you formulate an argument. But, it is wise to try to determine how well known and respected the treatise is, before you rely on it too heavily. Some treatises have been published for many, many years, in multiple editions. These are likely to be often used and well respected. Others are little more than one author's soapbox for espousing a point of view. Check with a librarian or with your legal colleagues if you are unsure about the level of respect accorded to a particular book.

Most law firms and legal departments have treatises on the topics relevant to their work. In such cases, you don't have to figure out which ones to use—they are at your fingertips. However, if you are looking for a treatise in a law library, you can do it through several means. Law libraries rarely have card catalogs of their holdings any more, but they usually do have online catalogs. Search the online catalog at a computer terminal for treatises by topic or by author. (You can do this in the library or from a remote location.) You will typically be given detailed information about the name of the book, its author, publisher, edition, date of publication, and so on. You will also be provided with a call number, so that you can find the book on the shelves. This number will typically begin with "KF" or "KFN," followed by a series of numbers. Go to the shelves in the library that are labeled "KF" or "KFN," and then search by number.

For example, suppose you are looking for a treatise on contract law. If you enter the topic "contracts" in the online catalog, you will probably get a huge number of possibilities. You can narrow your search by looking for specific topics or specific geographical areas within the topic, "contracts." If you want a general treatise from North Carolina, look for the sub-topic "North Carolina" within the topic "contracts." There, you may find a treatise entitled "North Carolina Contract Law" by John N.

Hutson and Scott A. Miskimon, carrying the call number, KFN7550 .H88. Or, if you want a treatise that has broader application, look for a book that covers contract law in the United States. There, you may find a "hornbook" (designed as a one-volume comprehensive summary, often used as a study aid by law students) called "Calamari and Perillo on Contracts." It carries the call number KF801 .C26. To find these books, go to the "stacks" in the library, find the KFN or KF section, where the books will be shelved in numerical order. Look for markers on shelves to pinpoint your search to KFN7550 for the North Carolina book, or KF801 for the national book. Then look within that area for ".H88" or C26. ("H" stands for Hutson, "C" for Calamari.)

If you are looking for a book and it is not on the shelf, be sure to check with the law librarian. Some books are so often used that they are kept on reserve, rather than in the stacks. Others are available in multiple copies, and the librarian may be able to direct you to a second copy in another area of the library.

Citing Treatises

Treatises are often hard to cite exactly. *The Bluebook* rule on the subject, R. 15, is detailed, and requires more information than many researchers think to note when they are looking at the book. Possible elements in a treatise citation include:

- volume number;
- 1st and 2nd authors' full names;
- full title of the book (possibly including the subtitle);
- section, paragraph, or page number(s) cited;
- editor and/or translator;
- edition;
- publisher;
- date.

The second example given in Rule 15.1(b) of *The Bluebook* is a fairly representative one for a treatise (modified below for practitioners):

14 Charles Alan Wright, Arthur R. Miller, & Edward H. Cooper, *Federal Practice and Procedure* § 3637 (3d ed. 1998).[1]

Assume that you are citing a particular point of law in a treatise, rather than the whole thing. Start your citation with the volume number of the treatise, if the treatise takes up more than one. For example, if you are citing something from the fourth volume of a multi-volume set, as in the example above, put the volume number, (here, "14") at the beginning of your cite.

Next give the name of the author(s), followed by a comma. If there is only one author, gives his or her full name as it appears on the title page of the book, e.g. "Joseph M. Perillo." If there are two authors, give both their names in the order they

---

1. *The Bluebook: A Uniform System of Citation* R. 15.1, at 130 (Columbia Law Review Ass'n et al. eds., 18th ed. 2005).

appear on the title page, separated by an ampersand ("&"), e.g., "Charles Alan Wright & Arthur R. Miller" If there are three or more authors, give the first author's full name, followed by "et al." (including the period after "al."), e.g., "A. Leo Levin et al." Alternatively, list all of the authors' names. Despite the large and small caps in *The Bluebook*, assuming you are a practitioner, convert everything to ordinary roman type.

Next comes the title of the treatise (also converted to ordinary type, and underlined or put in italics in accordance with the *Practitioners' Notes*). Ideally, the title won't be hard to determine, but often it is. Many treatises have both a main title and a subtitle. According to *The Bluebook,* "Give a subtitle only if it is particularly relevant."[2]

Sometimes, the author's name is included in the title, leaving you to wonder who the author is, and what the book is really called. This happens because books are often originally written by someone who becomes successful, authors multiple editions, and then retires or dies. Because the book is widely used and respected, its publisher chooses to keep it going by bringing in a new author (or authors) to revise the latest editions of the book. Sometimes the new author assists the original author before he or she leaves. All of this can result in confusion as to authors and titles and even editors. Be guided by the title page, and don't be afraid to include an author's name in the title. For example, "Joseph M. Perillo, Calamari and Perillo on Contracts...."

After the title comes the section, paragraph, or page number(s) on which the cited material can be found. If you are citing the whole treatise, you can omit this part. Otherwise, use either the section symbol (§) or paragraph symbol (¶) followed by the section or paragraph number, immediately after the title. If the book is not divided into sections or paragraphs, use the page number (without any symbols in front of it). Do not put a comma between the name of the title and the section, paragraph, or page number: "Joseph M. Perillo, Calamari and Perillo on Contracts § 9.4." For information on sections, paragraphs, and page numbers, see Rules 3.2 and 3.3 in *The Bluebook*.

Last comes parenthetical information. At a minimum, include the date the treatise was published in the parentheses. You also may need to identify the editor, translator, edition and/or publisher inside the parentheses in front of the date. Always include the editor and/or translator if there is one, followed by "ed." or "trans." If there is more than one editor or translator, follow the format for authors described in Rule 15.1: include the full name of all, or just the first one followed by "et al." if three or more. For example, your parentheses might include information like the example noted in *The Bluebook* under Rule 15.2: "(Harlon L. Dalton et al. eds., 1987)."[3] This indicates that there are three or more editors. Also indicate the edition you are citing, assuming there has been more than one: "(4th ed. 1992)." In general, you should seek to cite the most current edition, as it will contain the must up-to-date analysis.[4]

---

2. *Id.* R. 15.3, at 139.
3. *Id.* R. 15.2, at 131.
4. *Id.* R. 15.4, at 132.

Identify the publisher if it is not the original one: "Charles Dickens, <u>Bleak House</u> 59-55 (Norman Page ed., Penguin Books 1971) (1853)."[5] In this example, the first parenthetical phrase identifies the Norman Page **edition** and the publisher of the 1971 book as Penguin Books. Inside the second parentheses, the original publication date is identified as 1853. It sometimes may be difficult to determine when a book has had more than one publisher, but the library catalog can help. Given the consolidation of the legal publishing industry in recent years, the likelihood of having had multiple publishers is increasing.

Periodicals

Legal periodicals are publications that come out "periodically," i.e., at fixed intervals, typically four or more times per year. They usually are first published as a softbound pamphlet or magazine, but may later be consolidated into hardbound books. Legal periodicals include articles on various topics, often on current issues. Some periodicals are serious academic publications, like the law reviews and journals published by law schools, and can be relied upon in your research. Others are more practical, like a magazine published by a state bar and/or a professional association, or a legal newspaper, and are more useful as aids in the day-to-day practice of law.

Law Reviews and Journals

Most law schools publish at least one quarterly periodical called a "law review" or "law journal." These publications are well-respected sources of critical legal thinking. They typically include articles written by scholars such as law professors or lawyers who are expert in a particular area of law, notes or comments written by the top law students at the school, and reviews of recent cases or trends in the law, also written by the most academically advanced students.

North Carolina has five law schools, and each publishes a law review. In alphabetical order, these are:

- Campbell Law Review ("Campbell L. Rev.");
- Duke Law Journal ("Duke L.J.");
- North Carolina Central Law Journal ("N.C. Cent. L.J.");
- North Carolina Law Review ("N.C. L. Rev.");
- Wake Forest Law Review ("Wake Forest L. Rev.").

In addition, many of these schools publish other journals and reviews on particular legal topics. For example, the University of North Carolina School of Law publishes the "North Carolina Journal of International Law and Commercial Regulation" (N.C. J. Int'l L. & Com. Reg.") and Duke University School of Law publishes the "Duke Environmental Law & Policy Forum" ("Duke Envtl. L. & Pol'y F.") and

---

5. *Id.* at 132–133.

the "Duke Journal of Gender Law and Policy" ("Duke J. Gender L. Pol'y"), among others.

Finding Periodical Articles

To find an article in a periodical, whether an academic law review/journal, or a more practical article from a commercial magazine, newspaper, or association publication, you need an index just for periodicals. There are several. The best known and widely available are *Index to Legal Periodicals* ("I.L.P.") and *Current Law Index* ("C.L.I."). C.L.I. has a microfilm version called the *Legal Resources Index*. C.L.I. is also available on LEXIS and Westlaw, and through a computer-based service available in many law libraries called *LegalTrac*, a part of *InfoTrac*.

When you use the book indexes, you will see that they have some common characteristics. You can generally search them by author, subject, or sometimes title of the article, and you can also look up case names or statutes to find any articles written about them. Making a thorough search using these book indexes is time consuming. Each is initially published in a pamphlet form. All the pamphlets published in a year are "cumulated" together at the end of the year and published in a book, resulting in a separate index book for each year. However, the books are not cumulated, so you cannot go to one book, and find all the articles ever written on a particular subject. Rather, you must search year by year.

For example, assume you are looking for an article on automobile racetracks as nuisances. Look in the subject indexes for the most recent bound volume under "nuisances" and see what you find. Update your search by looking at the soft bound pamphlets which have not yet been cumulated and bound together into a hardbound volume. Then, depending upon how far back you want to go, pick up the volume for the prior year and make the same search, then the one for the year before that, and so on.

Often, because periodical articles are written on controversial or interesting topics of the day, you will not want to look at articles written too far back in time. Rather, you may prefer to have the most current thought and scholarship on the topic. In fact, it is unlikely that you would be asked to search 20 or 30 index books for the last 20–30 years of periodical articles. Occasionally, however, you will want to undertake a more thorough search. In those circumstances, a computer search is far easier.

For example, *LegalTrac* essentially cumulates articles appearing in the *Current Law Index*, allowing you to search from 1980 forward all at once. Simply enter the name of the author or subject and you will be directed to the applicable articles. There are mechanisms for narrowing your search, should you be given an overwhelming amount of information. Unfortunately, although *LegalTrac* is found in many law libraries, its use is sometimes limited to law students and faculty, or the members of that particular library. Ask a librarian for assistance if you cannot access it, and you may find that the librarian will allow you to use it.

Remember too that sometimes the best way to find a periodical is not through the index, but through other resources. Annotated statutory compilations, such as the *North Carolina General Statutes* or *North Carolina General Statutes Annotated*, and the U.S.C.A. and U.S.C.S., often reference law review articles about the statutes. And, secondary authorities like A.L.R. may also refer you to articles on point. You can also find them through computer-assisted research products like LEXIS and Westlaw (see chpt. 11), and through *Shepard's* (see chpt.10).

Citing Periodicals

Citation of legal periodicals is covered in *The Bluebook*, Rule 16. As usual, good examples are provided at the beginning of the rule. You are more likely to have to cite a law review or law journal article from an academic publication than an article from a commercial magazine. Use the first example as a guide for citing academic law reviews and journals:

Charles A. Reich, *The New Property*, 73 Yale L.J. 733, 737–38 (1964).

Note that the citation includes (in order) the:

- full name of the author followed by a comma,
- title of the article in italics (underlining is also acceptable) followed by a comma,
- volume number of the journal,
- abbreviated name of the journal (found in Table T. 14),
- page number on which the article begins followed by a comma,
- page numbers on which the referenced material is located, and
- year of the article in parentheses.

The specific rules for these components of the citation are spread out in Rule 16.

Pursuant to Rule 16.1, the **author** is cited the same way as authors of treatises under Rule 15.1: if one author, give his or her full name; if two authors, give both full names with an ampersand in between; and if three authors, give the full name of the first author followed by "et al." or the full name of all the authors.

The rules for citing the **title** are set out in Rule 16.2. Essentially, you should include the entire title as it appears on the title page of the journal article. Capitalize the first word no matter what, and every other word except the articles (e.g., "the," "a," "an"), conjunctions (e.g. "and," "but," "if"), and prepositions (e.g., "on," "in," "by") which are four letters long or less. (See Rule 8.)

Next you will describe the periodical you are citing. How you describe it depends upon whether or not it is "consecutively paginated." Law reviews and journals are consecutively paginated and fall under Rule 16.3. Magazines from bar associations and the like typically are not. Think of the magazines you subscribe to at home. Whether it's *Newsweek*, *Cosmopolitan*, or *Sports Illustrated*, one year's issues make up a "volume," and each issue begins on page 1. These magazines are nonconsecutively paginated. On the other hand, law reviews and journals usually are consecutively paginated. That means that, when the second issue of the year comes out, it begins on the next page after the last issue ended. Thus, if the January–March issue ended on page 502, the first page of the April–June issue will be page 503. The first issue of the next year's volume begins again at page 1.

Suppose you are citing a law review. It will almost certainly be consecutively paginated, bringing you to Rule 16.3. This rule requires that after you give the author and title of the article, you must give the volume number, abbreviated name of the law review or journal (see Table T.14), and the page number on which the article begins:

> Mitchell N. Berman, *Justification and Excuse, Law and Morality*, 53 Duke L.J. 1 (2003).

The above-cited article appears in volume 53 of the Duke Law Journal and begins on page 1.

If you are citing to something specific within the article, also give the page numbers on which that information appears:

> Mitchell N. Berman, *Justification and Excuse, Law and Morality*, 53 Duke L.J. 1, 39–58 (2003).

Only rarely will you cite a nonconsecutively paginated journal. Here, again, you will begin with author and title. However, you will next give the abbreviated name of the magazine followed by a comma, and then the "date of the issue as it appears on the cover, first page of work, and, if applicable, page or pages on which specific material appears following the word "at" (rule 3.2(a))."[6]

Sample Citation to a Non-Consecutively Paginated Journal/Magazine

Paul D. Carrington, *Selecting North Carolina Judges in the 21st Century*, N.C. St. B.J., Spring 2002, at 8.

American Law Reports ("A.L.R.")

American Law Reports ("A.L.R.") is a legal resource that publishes articles about recent noteworthy court decisions from across the country, both state and federal. It includes the decision itself (and thus, is in part primary authority), but more importantly, it thoroughly analyzes the decision and the legal issues raised therein.

---

6. *Id.* R. 16.4, at 140.

Reprinted with the permission of West, a Thomson Business.

For example, suppose you were asked to research a question about invasion of privacy by a newspaper. If you looked in the indexes to the various editions of the A.L.R. and found an article on point, you would have at your fingertips a wealth of information about the topic at hand: a case on this very subject, a complete article discussing it, references to cases, statutes, and other secondary authority from across the country, and references to other related A.L.R. articles, in case the article you found isn't exactly on point.

At the beginning of article, you will find a brief overview followed by a table of contents to help you find particular points within it. Cross references are listed to other resources, like Am. Jur., and a "table of jurisdictions represented" is provided so that you can see at a glance whether any North Carolina cases are presented.

Each article begins with an introductory "Scope" which tells you the legal question addressed, and then a summary of the article. The analysis that follows is from all sides, and describes how various states approach the issue. If states handle it differently, the article will break down the various approaches, and provide the point of view of the majority of states, and any minority points of view. Don't forget to check the supplement! There you will find any updates from the time the article was written through the date of publication of the supplement.

When you find an A.L.R. article on point, you are in the happy position of having a huge part of your research already done for you.

A.L.R. was first published in 1919 and was then called simply, "American Law Reports" or "A.L.R." Since then, there have been four additional editions—A.L.R.2d,

A.L.R.3d, A.L.R. 4th, and A.L.R. 5th—each about 100 volumes. A.L.R. and A.L.R.2d include both state and federal cases and analysis. Thereafter, analyses of federal court cases is published in a separate series called A.L.R. Fed.

A.L.R. is currently published by West, but was, until 1998, published by Lawyers Co-op. Thus, you will find slight variations between editions published by the two companies. For example, now that West owns A.L.R., it includes cross-references to its key number system which are absent from earlier editions. And, the cases now appear at the back of the volumes rather than immediately preceding the article.

Using A.L.R.

There are several indexes to help you find relevant A.L.R. articles. The most comprehensive is the *A.L.R. Index* which indexes all five editions of A.L.R. and the A.L.R. Fed. A shorter and easier (but obviously less comprehensive) index is the *A.L.R. Quick Index*. The *Quick Index* covers only the A.L.R. 3d and later editions, but since these are the most recent articles, it may be all that is necessary. In either index, look up your indexing words on the topic at hand. If you are researching a statute or rule, you can look it up in the index as well, and find any articles that cite it.

For the most comprehensive index, look to the A.L.R. digests. Like all digests, they are arranged alphabetically by subject. Once you have a good subject word, you can go straight to the digests and look up articles there. You will find more detailed summaries of each article than you will in the indexes.

The indexes and digests have supplements, or pocket parts, which you should also check for the most recent articles.

Citing A.L.R.

If you look up "A.L.R." in *The Bluebook* index, you won't find an entry. You have to know that it stands for "American Law Reports" or that it is an "Annotation." You will find an entry there, directing you to Rule 16.6.6, which gives you the rule and one example:

> Cite discussions in selective case reporters (such as *American Law Reports* and *Lawyer's Reports Annotated*) by the author's full name, followed by the designation "Annotation" in ordinary roman type and the title of the work in italics:

> William B. Johnson, Annotation, *Use of Plea Bargain or Grant of Immunity as Improper Vouching for Credibility of Witness in Federal Cases*, 76 A.L.R. Fed. 409 (1986).[7]

---

7. *Id.* R. 16.6.6, at 145.

Again, as practitioners, you must convert anything in all capital letters to ordinary roman type. Therefore, FED. Becomes "Fed." As usual, it is permitted to underline rather than to italicize.

Although most articles are written by a lawyer with the designation "J.D." after his or her name, this does not have to be included. But, be sure to include the word "Annotation," set off by commas, as it appears in the example. Although the title of each A.L.R. article is typically quite long, you must include the whole thing, set off by a comma. The number appearing before "A.L.R." is the volume number, and the number afterward is the page on which the annotation begins. If you cite to a particular page within the article, add it after the beginning page, set off by a comma:

> William B. Johnson, Annotation, *Use of Plea Bargain or Grant of Immunity as Improper Vouching for Credibility of Witness in Federal Cases*, 76 A.L.R. Fed. 409, 415 (1986).

Looseleaf Services

Looseleaf services are books, or series of books, published in looseleaf ring binders. They are designed to be a comprehensive resource on a particular area of law. Thus, they are a combination of primary authority (including cases, statutes and administrative regulations concerning their subject matter), secondary authority (including commentary, review of the law, and practical information about how to practice in this area), and finding tools (in that they reference other available information on the subject).

The advantages of looseleaf services are their comprehensive nature, and the speed with which they are updated. Looseleafs are updated constantly—not just once a year. Because the material is in a ring binder, the publisher can send substitute pages on a regular basis for pages that are no longer current, and additional pages for new information, with instructions on where to put them.

There are several different publishers of looseleaf services, including Commerce Clearinghouse and Matthew Bender. Consequently, not all looseleaf services are organized exactly the same way. However, they almost always have a section at the front of the first binder entitled, "How to Use this Book"—or something to that effect. In addition, they usually contain an index, table of contents, and colored tabs denoting the different sections of the book. Start with the instructions for a particular looseleaf and your research within it will be far more efficient in the long run.

Citing a Looseleaf Service

If you are citing a primary authority that you found in a looseleaf service, it is best to cite it to an official source, or a more commonly-held unofficial one. For example, suppose you find a federal statute in a looseleaf service. Instead of citing it to the looseleaf service, find and cite it to the U.S.C., U.S.C.A., or U.S.C.S. Similarly, cite the North Carolina General Statutes to the N.C. Gen. Stat. rather than to a looseleaf service, assuming you can check it in the General Statutes. Likewise, cite any cases to the official reporter, and/or an unofficial West reporter, as described in Table T.1 of *The Bluebook*. Remember that while statutes and reporters are widely available, looseleaf services are not.

If you do have to cite to a looseleaf, follow Rule 19.1 in *The Bluebook*. Unfortunately, because each service is different, each citation looks a little different. In general, you will want to identify any volume number, abbreviated title of the service (see Table T.15), the abbreviated name of the publisher (again see Table T.15 — a short list appears at the top of the table), the subdivision in which the material appears (e.g. section or paragraph number), and the date. This date should be exact if you are citing commentary or articles. *The Bluebook* gives this example cite for an article from Commerce Clearing House's Pension Plan Guide:

> *ERISA Preemption Bills Draw Praise from Labor and Criticism fomr Business,* [Aug. 1991–June 1993] Pens. Plan Guide (CCH) ¶ 26,263, at 27,037-10 (Aug. 2, 1991).[8]

Here, the title of the article is in italics. Next is essentially a volume number. According to *The Bluebook*, "[t]he volume designation of a service may be a number, a year, a descriptive subtitle from the volume's spine, or a combination of these...."[9] Next is the abbreviated name of the service, followed by the abbreviated name of the publisher in parens "(CCH)." After that, note the paragraph number in which the cited material is located, the page numbers on which it appears, and the specific date of the article in parentheses.

Other Secondary Sources

There are, of course, many other secondary sources beyond those described here. Some which you may encounter in your career include "Restatements" of the law on various subjects, uniform acts, form books, and even jury instructions. If you apply the skills you have already acquired researching other materials, you will have little trouble learning how to use these resources too. Citation rules for most of them are covered in *The Bluebook*.

---

8. *Id.* R. 19.1(d), at 163.
9. *Id.* R. 19.1(a), at 162.

Exercise 9 — Secondary Authority

1. Using *Strong's*, find a **1999** NC Supreme Court case holding that the NC *Residential Rental Agreements Act* is not applicable to a personal injury action by tenants against the homeowner because the home was not the plaintiff's primary residence and therefore there was no implied warranty of habitability.

   A. Cite the case.

   B. Give the citation to the section of *Strong's* where the case appears.

   C. What search terms did you use in the *Descriptive Word Index* to locate this section?

   D. Find and cite a case in the supplement on the same subject but involving an office supply company.

2. For additional background, use the *Descriptive Word Index* to *C.J.S.* and the *C.J.S.* "Landlord and Tenant" table of contents to find an entry discussing the right and duty of the **landlord** to repair in the absence of a statute or lease stipulation.

   A. Cite the *C.J.S.* entry.

   B. Is North Carolina listed with the jurisdictions that say that at common law, a lessor is not bound to make alterations to the leased property or repair it in the absence of an express covenant or stipulation?

3. Find and cite the entry in *Am. Jur.* dealing with the duty of a **tenant** to make repairs.

4. Using the *A.L.R. 3rd, 4th, 5th Quick Index,* find a 1980 *A.L.R.* annotation about damages for the landlord's breach of the implied warranty of habitability.

   A. Cite the annotation.

   B. Give the *Bluebook* citation to the Pennsylvania case that is the subject of the *A.L.R.* annotation.

   C. According to the *A.L.R.* annotation's **main volume only,** in a breach of warranty case, which states have held that where a tenant remains in possession of the premises, the tenant's damages may be measured by the difference between the fair rental value of the premises if they had been as warranted and their fair rental value during their occupancy by the tenant in the unfit condition?

   D. In the supplement for the Annotation, find a reference to pertinent *West Digest* key numbers. List the first one.

5. Using an on-line catalogue, locate *Webster's Real Estate Law* (a treatise). Cite the treatise.

6. Use the *Current Law Index* to locate a law review article the implied warranty of habitability in the 21st century. Cite the article.

Chapter 10

Shepard's Citations

Citators are books that help you determine the current validity of a primary authority and provide you with citations to other sources that have cited it. They are most commonly used to analyze whether a case is still "good law" or has been reversed, overturned, or criticized in some way. You can also use citators to determine the current validity of other authorities, including statutes, constitutions, certain administrative rules, court rules, executive orders, and more. In addition, citators are regularly used to find cases and other authorities that have cited a particular case, statute, administrative rule or other authority.

Use of *Shepard's North Carolina Citations*

The most widely used citator in book form (as opposed to electronic services) is called *Shepard's Citations*, published by LexisNexis. This series of books is so well known that you may be asked to "Shepardize" a case, i.e. to use *Shepard's Citations* to determine (1) is the case still "good law;" and (2) what cases and other authorities have cited the case you are "Shepardizing." An additional benefit of *Shepard's Citations* is that it also can be used to find parallel citations (see Chpt. 6). There are *Shepard's Citations* available for every state. North Carolina's is *Shepard's North Carolina Citations* ("*Shepard's*").

Using *Shepard's* in book form is not a straightforward task. First, you must make sure that you have all the necessary volumes of *Shepard's*, including various supplements. Next, you must learn to translate the information it provides into something meaningful. This takes practice, as the books do not contain any text. Instead, they consist entirely of columns of numbers and letters, as shown in Figure 10.1, a sample page from Shepard's North Carolina Citations.

NORTH CAROLINA REPORTS   **Vol. 310**

—308—

Case 3

Dolbow v
Holland
Industrial Inc.
1984

(312SE651)
s 64NCA695
95NCA622
98NCA462
99NCA303
100NCA123
j 100NCA129
107NCA754
110NCA234

—308—

Case 4

Kirks v Kirks
1984

(312SE651)
s 65NCA221

—308—

Case 5

McClure v
McClure
1984

(312SE651)
s 64NCA318
68NCA182
81NCA69
81NCA283
83NCA11
100NCA23
39A1072n

—309—

Case 1

Misenheimer v
Misenheimer
1984

(312SE651)
s 62NCA706

—309—

Case 2

News &
Observer v
North Carolina
1984

(312SE652)
s 65NCA576

—309—

Case 3

Roper v
J.P. Stevens
& Co.
1984

(312SE652)
s 65NCA69
70NCA755
71NCA379
71NCA788
78NCA414
79NCA73
83NCA104
84NCA82
106NCA43

—309—

Case 4

Sasser v Beck
1984

(312SE652)
s 65NCA170
78NCA598
82NCA433
84NCA325

—309—

Case 5

North Carolina
v Alexander
1984

(312SE653)
s 65NCA221

—310—

Case 1

North Carolina
v Hinnant
1984

(312SE653)
s 65NCA130
319NC455
77NCA525
79NCA442
86NCA322
101NCA45
101NCA322
28WFL547

—310—

Case 2

North Carolina
v Langley
1984

(312SE653)
s 64NCA674

—310—

Case 3

North Carolina
v Proctor
1984

(312SE654)
s 62NCA233

—310—

Case 4

North Carolina
v Simmons
1984

(312SE654)
s 64NCA727
89NCA205

—310—

Case 5

North Carolina
v Smith
1984

(312SE648)
s 65NCA222

—311—

Case 1

North Carolina
v Summerford
1984

(312SE654)
s 65NCA519
80NCA47

—311—

Case 2

North Carolina
v Taylor
1984

(312SE655)
s 63NCA364
cc 322NC433
cc 85NCA549
95NCA45

—312—

Renwick
v News and
Observer
Publishing Co.
1984

(312SE405)
(57A1)
US cert den
in 469US858
in 105SC187
Cert Den
s 310NC749
s 63NCA200
f 323NC6263
e 323NC6271
326NC3223
326NC4223
j 326NC228
j 334NC207
70NCA360
72NCA643
78NCA674
78NCA4675
78NCA6761
84NCA311
84NCA1133
84NCA2133
e 85NCA6614
89NCA4525
91NCA4181
103NCA2771
109NCA1274
111NCA277
113NCA706
114NCA4534
Cir. 4
620FS1383
722FS1314
827FS4352
843FS62
843FS63
843FS64
843FS67
Cir. 7
769F2d61133
Cir. 8
e 786FS6797
63NCL767
64NYL368
59A4512n
59A4547n
60A484n
60A6166n
62A6568n

—332—

North Carolina
v Stanley
1984

(312SE393)
310NC1494
j 310NC504
f 312NC1175

j 312NC179
f 315NC1433
d 315NC434
317NC1394
j 319NC28
319NC1146
d 320NC1222
320NC1694
f 321NC1319
d 325NC1317
329NC180
332NC469
j 332NC519
f 335NC61
d 335NC63
335NC3
336NC373
78NCA147
64NCL975
63A4587n

—353—

North Carolina
v Stanley
1984

(312SE482)
311NC6743
312NC3768
313NC88
317NC8435
320NC3122
321NC136
334NC487
89NCA6219
36MJ168

—369—

North Carolina
v Thomas
1984

(312SE458)
316NC2409
318NC1247
j 325NC346
f 73NCA1550
81NCA1626
88NCA1202
d 88NCA1467
101NCA1600
106NCA552
113NCA224
63NCL1214
20WFL25
27A31431s
18A4360s

—384—

North Carolina
v Watson
1984

(312SE448)
311NC3498
312NC6296

312NC2507
316NC2512
316NC7692
317NC17
317NC2198
317NC5205
e 317NC5608
317NC1634
e 318NC50
320NC478
321NC6140
322NC500
323NC691
323NC6284
327NC6356
f 331NC3166
332NC400
332NC465
332NC1468
332NC6596
334NC6228
f 69NCA698
j 74NCA31
77NCA144
111NCA317
33A317s
34A31256s
74A4338n
74A4342n
74A4348n

—399—

North Carolina
v Alston
1984

(312SE470)
s 61NCA454
d 315NC1747
316NC519
d 318NC2656
j 318NC662
L 319NC44
L 319NC245
j 319NC51
319NC2614
321NC673
d 323NC1354
d 332NC2267
d 332NC1268
f 70NCA760
f 70NCA2760
j 70NCA762
74NCA1467
j 76NCA59
77NCA818
79NCA2200
80NCA704
82NCA2598
85NCA2516
f 89NCA2683
d 89NCA1684
90NCA533
d 92NCA2427

Continued

595

Figure 10.1   Reprinted with the permission of LexisNexis.

Necessary Volumes of *Shepard's* to Determine the Current Validity of a Case

When using *Shepard's* to determine the current validity of a case, you will find a number of related volumes on the shelf, both hardbound and softbound. You will need several different books to do a complete search, and it is important to have all the right ones.

In order to assure that you are provided the most up-to-date information possible, *Shepard's* is supplemented far more often than many law books. There are, of course, main volumes (maroon in color). There is also a hardbound supplement (also maroon). In addition, there are several softbound supplements: typically an annual cumulative supplement (gold) and a monthly supplement (red). Because you use *Shepard's* to determine the current validity of a case or other authority, it is important that you check all the available supplements up to the time you are doing your research. Wouldn't you want to know if a case came out last week that reverses the one you were hoping to use in an argument before a court? You cannot afford to wait for an annual supplement—you need to know the status of your case now.

To determine if you have a complete set of volumes to "Shepardize" a case, pick up the latest advance sheet or supplement you can find. This should be a red pamphlet, if the set is supplemented monthly. (However, you may find an even more current supplement if the subscriber to your service has paid for additional updates.) At any rate, the latest supplement should be the thinnest one on the shelf. Check the month and year of this pamphlet. These should be the same month and year as it is at the time you are doing your research, or the month before. Thus, if you are doing your research in October, the pamphlet should be dated October or September. If the most current supplement is any older than that, check with the librarian about the location of a more recent pamphlet.

Once you are sure that you have the most recent supplement, look at the front cover where it reads, "What your library should contain." Make sure you have each item on the list. These should include:

- the 1995 bound volumes for North Carolina cases (volumes 1–4);
- a 1995–2000 bound supplement supplementing the bound volumes;
- a gold annual cumulative supplement going forward from the date of the bound supplement;
- a red cumulative supplement including material subsequent to the gold; and
- perhaps an additional supplement including material subsequent to the red.

The last entry on the list should be for the pamphlet you have in your hand, which should be the red monthly supplement or one that is even more current.

Decoding the Entries in *Shepard's*

Once you have a complete set of *Shepard's* you are ready to start. At first glance, a page from Shepard's looks unintelligible. Look back at Figure 10.1. It includes several columns, with occasional numbers in bold, followed by case names, a year, and then a series of individual entries. In general, each entry in each column refers to a different case or other authority. These authorities will fall into one of six categories:

(1) a parallel cite for the case you are Shepardizing;
(2) the history of the particular case you are Shepardizing through the court system;
(3) other cases that cite the case you are Shepardizing ("citing cases");
(4) opinions of the Attorney General that cite the case you are Shepardizing;
(5) legal periodicals that cite the case you are Shepardizing; and
(6) annotations (A.L.R. articles) that cite the case you are Shepardizing.

How do you get all this information out of the series of columns of combined letters and numbers? First, look at the individual entries in each column closely. You may find that they look somewhat familiar. For example, at the top of the last column on the right of the sample Shepard's page, you will see "312NC^{2}507." As you might guess, this refers to a case printed in volume 312 of the *North Carolina Reports,* page 507. It is simply a squeezed-together version of the citation, "312 N.C. 507" which you already know how to find. (See chapter 5.) (For information on the superscript number "2," see "Treatment of a Case" below.)

Suppose you see instead something like the very last entry in the last column of the sample page: "d 92NCA^{2}427." This, of course, refers to volume 92 of the North Carolina Court of Appeals reporter at page 427. It is a shorthand version of the citation, "92 N.C. App. 427." (For information about the "d" preceding the cite, see "Letter Codes Preceding Entries" below.)

On each line, the number on the left side of the capital letters is a volume number, while the number on the right is a page number. The letters in between abbreviate the resource cited.

Common Case-Related Abbreviations in *Shepard's*

There are abbreviations pages at the front of every *Shepard's* outlining all the abbreviations contained in the volume. The most common entries for **reported cases** in a North Carolina *Shepard's* are:

"NC"	*N.C. Reports*
"NCA"	*N.C. Court of Appeals Reports*
"SE"	*South Eastern Reporter*
"SE"	*South Eastern Reporter, 2nd Series*—the "2" is squashed inside the "E"

"FS"	*Federal Supplement*
"FS2d"	*Federal Supplement 2nd*
"F"	*Federal Reporter*
"F2d"	*Federal Reporter, 2nd Series*
"F3d"	*Federal Reporter, 3rd Series*
"Cir. 4"	Fourth Circuit, U.S. Court of Appeals
"US"	*United States Reports* (official U.S. Supreme Court case reporter)
"SC"	(United States) *Supreme Court Reporter* (published by West)
"LE"	*United States Supreme Court Reports, Lawyers' Edition*

For cases that are so recent that they are not yet published in a reporter, *Shepard's* cross-references LEXIS—a computer-assisted legal research product. In such cases, the most common entries you will see relating to LEXIS are:

"LX"	LEXIS
"NCApp"	North Carolina Court of Appeals
"NC"	North Carolina Supreme Court
"USDist"	Federal (U.S.) District Court
"USApp"	Federal (U.S.) Court of Appeals

Abbreviations to Other Resources in *Shepard's*

Other resources commonly cited in *Shepard's* include periodicals and annotations from American Law Reports that cite North Carolina cases. You will often see abbreviations such as these :

"NCL"	North Carolina Law Review
"WFL"	Wake Forest Law Review
"DuLJ"	Duke Law Review
"NCC"	NCCU Law Review
"AL3"	A.L.R. 3d (entry will be stylized)
"AL4"	A.L.R. 4th (entry will be stylized)
"ALF"	A.L.R. Federal (entry will be stylized).

Letter Codes Preceding Entries

What about the lower case letters that appear in front of some of the case citations, e.g. "s" or "f" or "j?" These are explained on the "ABBREVIATIONS—ANALYSIS" page at the front of each volume of *Shepard's Citations*. (See Figure 10.2 below.) They tell you particular information about the **history of a case** through the court system, and how it has been **treated** by other later cases. To fully understand these letters, you must understand the distinction between the "History of [a] Case" and the "Treatment of [a] Case."

CASES ANALYSIS–ABBREVIATIONS

History of Case

a	(affirmed)	Same case affirmed on appeal.
cc	(connected case)	Different case from case cited but arising out of same subject matter or intimately connected therewith.
D	(dismissed)	Appeal from same case dismissed.
De	(denied)	Petition for discretionary review, certiorari, rehearing or reconsideration denied.
Gr	(granted)	Petition for discretionary review, certiorari, rehearing or reconsideration granted.
m	(modified)	Same case modified on appeal.
r	(reversed)	Same case reversed on appeal.
s	(same case)	Same case as case cited.
S	(superseded)	Substitution for former opinion.
v	(vacated)	Same case vacated.
W	(withdrawn)	Same case withdrawn.
US cert den		Certiorari denied by U. S. Supreme Court.
US cert dis		Certiorari dismissed by U. S. Supreme Court.
US reh den		Rehearing denied by U. S. Supreme Court.
US reh dis		Rehearing dismissed by U. S. Supreme Court.
US app pndg		Appeal pending before the U. S. Supreme Court.

Treatment of Case

c	(criticized)	Soundness of decision or reasoning in cited case criticized for reasons given.
ca	(conflicting authorities)	Among conflicting authorities as noted in cited case.
d	(distinguished)	Case at bar different either in law or fact from case cited for reasons given.
e	(explained)	Statement of import of decision in cited case. Not merely a restatement of the facts.
f	(followed)	Cited as controlling.
h	(harmonized)	Apparent inconsistency explained and shown not to exist.
j	(dissenting	Citation in dissenting opinion.
L	(limited)	Refusal to extend decision of cited case beyond precise issues involved.
o	(overruled)	Ruling in cited case expressly overruled.
op	(overruled) in part)	Ruling in cited case partially or on other grounds or with other qualifications.
p	(parallel)	Citing case substantially alike or on all fours with cited case in its law or facts.
q	(questioned)	Soundness of decision or reasoning in cited case questioned.
su	(superseded))	Superseded by statute as stated in cited case.
~	(concurring)	Citation in concurring opinion.
#		The citing case is questionable precedential value because review or rehearing has been granted by the California Supreme Court and/or the citing case has been ordered depublished pursuant to Rule 976 of the California Rules of Court. (Publication Status should be verified before use of the citing case in California.)

Figure 10.2   Reprinted with the permission of LexisNexis.

"History" vs. "Treatment" of a Case

You can see from Figure 10.2 that the abbreviations page of *Shepard's* is divided into two parts: "History of Case" and "Treatment of Case." This is a critical distinction. The **history of a case** covers citations to the case you are Shepardizing as it has worked its way through the court system. On the other hand, the **treatment of a case** involves other later cases that have cited your case in their opinions. These other cases may have cited your case either favorably or unfavorably.

History of a Case

Assume that the case of <u>Simon v. ABC Co.</u> was tried in civil superior court in Wake County. Simon won, and ABC Co. appealed. The appeal was heard by the North Carolina Court of Appeals, which upheld the trial court's decision. ABC Company petitioned the Supreme Court for certiorari, which heard the appeal and reversed the Court of Appeals and trial court. Simon petitioned the United States Supreme Court to hear the case, but his petition was denied.

In this scenario, the case of <u>Simon v. ABC Co.</u> has now been considered in some form by four different courts: the Superior Court, Court of Appeals, N.C. Supreme Court and U.S. Supreme Court. Although you cannot find the Superior Court's decision in a traditional reporter, you can find all three appellate versions (Court of Appeals, N.C. Supreme Court, and U.S. Supreme Court). You can also look up each appellate court decision in *Shepard's*.

No matter which of the three appellate versions of <u>Simon v. ABC Co.</u>, you look up in *Shepard's* (Court of Appeals, Supreme Court or US Supreme Court), it will include cross references to the other two appellate opinions in that case in the column of numbers beneath the citation with which you started, in chronological order. Each one of these cross-references to **other appellate decisions in the same case** is considered "history." The opinions that occurred before the one you look up are considered "prior history," and those that came after it are considered "subsequent history." In general, what you will care about most is subsequent history. **Subsequent history** is everything that happened in your case after the decision you are Shepardizing, including the courts' decisions on all subsequent appeals and petitions to consider or reconsider the case.

Often, you can determine whether a listed case is part of the history of the case you are researching by looking at the letter-abbreviations that precede it. Citations for your case's history will nearly always be preceded by an abbreviation from the list on the first half of the *Shepard's* Abbreviations page (Figure 10.2). If it doesn't have one of the listed abbreviations, it is probably not history, but treatment.

Treatment of a Case

After any entries for the history of a case, you will find entries for other authorities that cite yours, including cases, law reviews and A.L.R. articles, in that order.

The "citing cases" will involve different parties than yours. However, the facts and/or issues in your case, and the citing cases, are likely to be similar. This is what makes *Shepard's* a helpful research tool: you can look up the cases that cite your case, and find others like it that address the same legal issues. If you look closely, you will find that in the *Shepard's North Carolina Citations*, the state supreme court citing cases come first, then the court of appeals cases, and then the federal cases. The federal cases from the 4th Circuit Court of Appeals and federal district courts in the 4th circuit come before cases from other circuits. Within each court, the citing cases will be ordered chronologically.

You can also find law review articles, Attorney General opinions (rarely) and A.L.R. articles that have cited your case. These citing authorities could be from across the state or country, and are likely to address similar issues to those in your case. You may even find a detailed analysis of your case in some of the citing authorities.

Sometimes it is hard to determine where history ends in the *Shepard's* list, and treatment begins. While history is nearly always preceded by a letter code, treatment may or may not be. Certainly, any case that is preceded by a letter code from the **second half** of the list on the Abbreviations page is **treatment**. Look back to Figure 10.2 for the list of possible abbreviations. For example, if you see a citation preceded by the letter "c," you will know that the cited case is not part of the history of your case, but instead is a separate case that **criticizes** the one you are Shepardizing

Another indication that a case is "treatment" rather than "history" lies in the **superscript numbers** you find in many of the citations. For example, look at the last column of numbers in Figure 10.1. The first entry reads, "$312NC^2507$." Whenever you see a small "superscript" number, like the "2" (raised above the regular type), this case is "treatment," that is, a separate case from the one you are Shepardizing.

As for the raised "2," it means that the case in the list concerns the same topic as the **second headnote** in the case you are Shepardizing. Thus, if you are interested in finding cases that cover the same topic as that in headnote number 2 of your case, you can scan the list of citing cases and authorities, and look up only those that include the superscript number "2." Each of these will be on the same topic as headnote number "2" in your case. And, the page number provided will be the place in the citing case that addresses the same topic as the second headnote in your case (not the first page of the case).

"Shepardizing" to Determine Whether a Case Is "Good Law"

Suppose that in your research, you have come across a helpful case. Before you can rely on the law handed down in that decision, you must determine whether it is "good law," that is, whether it may be relied on as precedent. Has the losing party appealed? Might the court reconsider its decision? Is a higher court going to look at the case, or has one already looked at it and reversed, modified, or superceded it? Any of these possibilities in the **history** of the case could affect its value as precedent.

Likewise, if other cases have **treated** your case in a negative way, this too can impact on its validity. For example, if a separate court of equal or higher standing in the same jurisdiction has overruled your case, it is not good law. And, even if your case has been merely questioned or criticized by another court, that too indicates the case may not be the best one on which to rely.

Thus, you need to check out the subsequent history of the case, to make sure it is the final decision in the matter. You also need to know if any other cases that have come after yours call the decision of your case into question. You can find out by looking up the case in *Shepard's*. The process is called "Shepardizing."

First, you must find the right volume of *Shepard's* with which to begin. This depends upon the reporter in which it appears, and the year of decision. If you are researching a North Carolina appellate opinion, you can Shepardize it using its citation to the official or unofficial reporter.

Match your citation to the volume of *Shepard's* in which it appears. Start with the earliest volume of *Shepard's* in which the case could appear. For example, if the decision precedes 1995, start with the original 1995 hardbound volumes of *Shepard's*. If the case you are Shepardizing was decided between 1995 and 2000, start with the one-volume hardbound supplement. And, if it was even more recent, look in the gold or red supplement.

Be sure that you are using the book of *Shepard's* containing citations to the reporter you are using, and that you are in the right section of that book. Some volumes contain more than one reporter. Always look at the header running across the top of the page to be sure that you are in the right place. For example, if you are starting with a cite to the North Carolina Supreme Court case, the header at the top of the relevant Shepard's page should say, "*NORTH CAROLINA REPORTS*." Assuming you are starting with the S.E.2d, it should reference the South Eastern Reporter, 2d Series across the top.

Once you are in the correct volume of *Shepard's* for your reporter, look in the outer, upper corner of the pages for the volume number of the reporter that corresponds with the case you are Shepardizing. For example, if you have a case in volume 310 of the *Supreme Court Reports*, look for the number "310" in the outer upper corners of the pages, as shown in Figure 10.1.

After you reach the correct volume number in the upper corner, scan the pages for the bold page number on which your case begins. These numbers are in a slightly larger font than the other entries in the book. For example, if your case begins on page 312 of volume 310 of the *Supreme Court Reports*, then you are looking for a bold "312" centered in a column on a page with 310 in the upper, outer corner.

Practice Set 10.1

Look at the sample *Shepard's* page reprinted as Figure 10.1. Can you find the case reported in 310 N.C. 312? Can you find the case cited in 310 N.C. 384?

What is the name of the case beginning on page 384? _____

When was it decided? _____

Immediately below the bold page number, the name of the case will be provided, followed by the year of decision. This information helps you verify that you are in the right place. If you cannot find the bold page number on which your case begins, or the case name doesn't match yours, double check to be sure you are in the volume and section of *Shepard's* that covers the reporter you are using, and make sure that the case hasn't appeared in an earlier edition of *Shepard's*.

After the case name and the year of decision is a column of citations to other authorities. The first entry for any case you look up is likely to be the parallel citation, in parentheses, to the same decision as printed in another reporter. If you start with a citation to the *North Carolina Reports* or the *North Carolina Court of Appeals Reports*, then the first entry will be a cross-reference to the parallel citation in the *South Eastern Reporter*, or *South Eastern Reporter, 2nd Series*. If instead, you start with the citation to the *South Eastern Reporter*, then the first entry will be a cross-reference to the same case in the official reporter. Some cases may also have a second parallel citation to the A.L.R. That means the case is also reprinted there. Remember that each parallel citation will always be in parentheses. If a citation is not in parentheses, then it is not the parallel cite to the case you are looking up.

Note

The first time a case appears in *Shepard's*, its name and parallel citation will be provided (if there is a parallel citation—remember, most federal cases don't have one). Thereafter, neither the parallel cite nor the name will appear. For instance, if a case was decided in 1999, it will first appear in *Shepard's* hardbound supplement, which covers 1995–2000. The case name and parallel cite will appear there. The case will not appear at all in the main volumes—it didn't exist at the time they were published. If there is case history, or treatment, after the date the hardbound supplement was published, this will appear in the softbound supplements. However, neither the name of the case nor the parallel citation will be repeated in the supplements. If you see an entry for a case in any supplement that does not include the case name and parallel citation, this means that the case has been addressed in at least one prior iteration of *Shepard's*. Thus, if you are beginning the process of Shepardizing a case, you are not in the right volume!

The next entry after the parenthetical parallel cite(s) will be any **prior history**. Of course, if you are Shepardizing a Court of Appeals case, it is likely that there will be no reported prior history. In most cases, the only decision that precedes a Court of Appeals case will be an unreported Superior Court case. (The Superior Court's decision is not published in a reporter and therefore is not referenced in *Shepard's*.) If you are Shepardizing a North Carolina Supreme Court decision, the reported prior history will normally be just the Court of Appeals' decision. The next entry will be to any subsequent history.

Remember that the abbreviations **in front of** each entry will help you determine (1) whether it is part of the case history, or treatment; and (2) if history, whether it is prior history, or subsequent history. Remember too that to help you separate history from treatment, *Shepard's* divides its abbreviations page into two parts. The first half of the abbreviations are devoted to history and the second half to treatment.

For example, if an entry has an "a" in front of it, this means that the case cited there "**affirmed**" the case you are Shepardizing. An affirmation of your case must have been made after the decision you have in your hand, and is therefore **subsequent** history. Likewise, if an entry has a "D" **dismissing** your case, an "m" **modifying** that case, an "r" **reversing** it, an "S" **superseding** your case, a "v" **vacating** your case, or a "US cert den," "US cert. dis," "US reh den," or "US reh dis," indicating the United States Supreme Court **declined** to **grant certiorari** or **rehear** the case, you can surmise that these events happened after the decision you are Shepardizing, and are therefore subsequent history.

Other entries for history are more equivocal: "cc" for "connected case" simply tells you that the case arises out of the same facts as yours; and "s" merely indicates that it is the "same case" as the one you are looking up. Typically, however, a citation with an "s" in front of it is a decision from a court lower than the one you are looking up, and is **prior history**.

Once you have sorted out the prior history from the subsequent history, you must analyze the subsequent history to determine if any of it calls your case into question. Certainly, if the opinion you are Shepardizing has been reversed, superceded, or vacated, you should not rely on it. That opinion is no longer "good law." Likewise, if the decision has been modified, that decision is suspect. You must look at the modifications made by the subsequent court to determine how it affects the decision in your case.

On the other hand, if your case has been "affirmed" by a higher court, or the higher courts have declined to hear it, then the case appears to be good law, so far. If a higher court has granted certiorari, or a petition to hear or rehear the case, then its outcome is not final, and caution is in order.

Next, look at the treatment of the case. Check for any case that criticizes, limits, questions, or overrules yours. If your case has been overruled, that's bad news. It is no longer "good law." If it has been criticized, limited, or questioned, then it is suspect. You must look at these decisions to determine how they affect your case.

Other types of treatment are equivocal. For example, a case that distinguishes or harmonizes its opinion with yours at least leaves your decision intact. However, these cases are worthy of review, in that they may indicate that the holding in your case should not be broadly applied. Cases that follow your case, cite it in a dissenting opinion, or explain it, are probably not of concern. Likewise, cases with no lower-case letters preceding them are not of concern either. These are cases that merely cite your case, and are likely to be favorable or neutral.

After you have found all the subsequent history and treatment that could impact the validity of your case in the *Shepard's* volume you have in front you, you must update your findings in all subsequent supplements. The supplements may have additional cases that affect whether or not your case is "good law."

For example, if you started with the main volume, then you must check at least three supplements: the hardbound, the gold and the red. If there is an additional supplement beyond those in your library, check it too. Your case will appear in each supplement only if a case was decided during the time frame covered by the supplement that is part of your case's history, or cites your case. Thus, it is possible that there will be no entry in a supplement to your case. Even if there isn't an entry in one supplement, that doesn't mean there won't be entries in subsequent supplements, so don't skip any.

Computer-Assisted Case Validation

If Sheparizing seems like a complex process, it is. This is one area where computers have eased the job significantly. *Shepard's* is available through LEXIS's computer assisted legal research, and is much easier there. Similarly, Westlaw offers KeyCite®, a comparable service which also simplifies the process. In either case, you click on the appropriate icon to Shepardize or validate your case, and you will be advised of the prior history, subsequent history, any negative treatment, and other citing cases and authorities. Links to each of these is provided.

Sample Sheparizing:
Renwick v. News & Observer

Assume you are Shepardizing the case of <u>Renwick v. News and Observer Publishing Co.</u>, 310 N.C. 312, 312 S.E.2d 405 (1984). The relevant page from the main volume of *Shepard's* appears in Figure 10.1. If you had the page from this volume in front of you (and you weren't reading this book), it would mean you started with the official cite: 310 N.C. 312. You looked for the volumes covering cases in 1985, and found that they appear in the main volumes. Then, you picked the volume covering the *North Carolina Reports*, including its volume 310. Then, you searched for volume 310 in the upper, outer corners of the *Shep-*

ard's pages, and once there, narrowed your search to the bold 312, the beginning page of the case. All this would have led you to the sample page in *Shepard's* reprinted above.

Go to Figure 10.1 and find the case caption *"Renwick v. News and Observer Publishing Co."* in the 4th column of *Shepard's*. Following down the list, note that the first entry is "1984," the year of the decision in the case. Next is "(312SE405)." This is the parallel cite to the same case in the *South Eastern Reporter, 2d Series*. Immediately thereafter is "(57A㸠1)." This, too, is a parallel cite. It must be, because it is inside parentheses. The case is reprinted in volume 57 of the A.L.R. 4th at page 1. There is an article in that A.L.R. addressing the subject matter of *Renwick* (false light invasion of privacy).

Next is history, beginning with:

US cert den
in 469US858
in 105SC187.

Remember, "US cert den" is an abbreviation from the "history" portion of the list. This means the United States Supreme Court denied *certiorari* in the *Renwick* case, in volume 469 U.S. 858 and volume 105 S. Ct. 187. These two entries are parallel citations, i.e., cites to the same opinion in two parallel U.S. Supreme Court reporters. Were you to look up the case in either of these two reporters, you would find a very short entry including the case caption, date of decision, and one sentence indicating the Court declined to take the case.

Following the parallel U.S. Supreme Court entries is an entry to the North Carolina Supreme Court:

Cert Den
s310NC749.

Is this history, or treatment? You can tell it is history because the case cite is preceded by two abbreviations from the "history" section: "Cert Den" and "s." The North Carolina Supreme Court declined to consider the case and its statement declining to do so is found in volume 310 on page 749. Of course, the Supreme Court already took up the matter once, in the case you are Shepardizing (310 N.C. 312). Yet, here is another entry to the case only 400-plus pages later in the same reporter! If you look it up, you will find that the losing party petitioned the North Carolina Supreme Court to reconsider its decision, but that the Supreme Court declined to do so. This entry is short, like the U.S. Supreme Court's decision, since the substance of the case was not considered.

The next entry is, "s 63NCA200." Is it history? Yes, since it is preceded by the lower case, "s" for "same case." This case is from the Court of Appeals ("NCA"), so you can guess that it is prior history. In fact, this is the first appellate decision in *Renwick* after the trial, but before it made it to the Supreme Court whose opinion you are Shepardizing. If you look it up, you can verify that this is so. It is easy to tell, because the date of this opinion precedes the date of the Supreme Court opinion.

The next entry is, "f 323NC⁶263." Is this history? No. You can tell from two different cues: first, the case is preceded by a lower case "f," meaning "followed," an abbreviation from the treatment section of *Shepard's*. Second, the entry includes superscript: the number "6" just after "NC." This means that it is a citing case that "follows" *Renwick*. It discusses the point covered in the sixth headnote of *Renwick*, beginning on page 263 of the citing case. If you look up the case in volume 323 of the *Supreme Court Reports* and go to its page 263, you will find *Renwick* cited there.

Since the entry, "f 323NC⁶263" turned out to be treatment, you can now safely assume that everything that follows in the list is treatment, i.e., cases, then other authorities, that cite and discuss the case of *Renwick*. Indeed, the next entry, "e 323NC⁶271," is treatment, and turns out to be the same case cited immediately above it. This case again cites *Renwick*, again on the same topic as is covered by *Renwick's* sixth headnote (in the official version), but this time on page 271. If you go to page 271 of the case in volume 323, you will find a second cite to *Renwick*.

Next are two entries to a case in volume 326 of the *North Carolina Reports*, both on page 223. One carries a superscript "3" and the other a superscript "4," meaning that the points addressed in the third and fourth headnote of *Renwick*, in the official reporter, are mentioned in the case listed, on page 223.

A lower case "j" precedes the next two entries, meaning *Renwick* is cited in dissenting opinions in the volumes and pages given. These two cases end the series of entries for North Carolina Supreme Court citing cases. The next entries are for cases from the North Carolina Court of Appeals. These entries work just like the Supreme Court entries. The superscript numbers refer to the *Renwick* headnotes in the official reporter. The entry, "e 85NCA⁶614" means that the case in volume 85 of the N.C. App. explains *Renwick*, and that it does so on page 614. You will find *Renwick* cited on that page.

A little further down the list, you will see an indented, "Cir. 4" followed by "620FS1383." This is a **Federal Supplement** case from a federal district court (from which appeal will be to the fourth circuit). All the following cases are too, until you get to "Cir. 8." The case after that is again a *Federal Supplement* case, but with appeal to the Eighth (8th) Circuit.

Immediately after the 8th Circuit case is the entry "63NCL767." This is an entry to the *North Carolina Law Review*, volume 63, page 767, where *Renwick* is cited. Next is an entry to the *New York Law Review* where *Renwick* is also cited. Finally, you see five entries to the A.L.R. Since these are not in parentheses, they are not parallel citations. Rather, they are five entries to three articles, all in the A.L.R. 4th, that reference *Renwick* on the pages given. The lower case "n" simply means that *Renwick* is cited in the annotation.

Looking back at the list of entries, do you see any that call into question the validity of *Renwick*? It has been followed and explained and cited in a dissenting opinion, but nothing appears reversing it or overturning it or otherwise calling it into question. Further, it does not appear from the entries that a court is currently considering an appeal. Thus, it looks like good law. But what is left undone? Remember, to fully Shepardize the case, you must check each supplement to see if it appears therein, and, if any of the entries call the decision into question. If you did, you would find that *Renwick* was later criticized twice: once by the Colorado Court of Appeals in 2000, and again by the Tennessee Supreme Court in 2001.

Practice Set 10.2

Using just the sample Shepard's page reprinted in this chapter as Figure 10.1, Shepardize the case of *North Carolina v. Hinnant*, 310 N.C. 10, for the following:

1. What is the parallel citation?

2. Is there any subsequent history? If so, list the citation(s):

3. Is there any prior history? If so, list the citation(s):

4. Give a full *Bluebook* citation to *Hinnant*, including any subsequent history:

5. What is the first entry in the "treatment" section?

6. How many citing cases are listed from the Supreme Court? _____
   Court of Appeals? _____

7. What does the last entry in the list mean?

8. According to just the *Shepard's* page depicted in Figure 1, is the *Hinnant* case good law?

Exercise 10 — Sheypardizing

Using *Shepard's Citations*, determine whether each case listed is still "good law." If not, give the complete citation of the case that affected it in accordance with *Bluebook* rules (including 10.2.1 and 10.2.2). Also, state how the later decision affected your precedent case. Include cases that clearly show your case is not good law, and those that call it into question, limit it, modify it, or the like. If the case is good law, simply answer, "good law."

Example: <u>Threadgill v. Town of Wadesboro</u>, 170 N.C. 641, 87 S.E. 521 (1916)

Response: Questioned by <u>Rowan County Bd. of Educ. v. United States Gypsum Co.</u>, 332 N.C. 1, 418 S.E.2d 648 (1992)

1. <u>Kimberly v. Howland</u>, 143 N.C. 399, 55 S.E. 778 (1906)

2. <u>Butler v. Butler</u>, 169 N.C. 584, 86 S.E. 507 (1915)

3. <u>Mial v. Ellington</u>, 134 N.C. 131, 46 S.E. 961 (1903)

4. <u>State v. Harrison</u>, 90 N.C. App. 629, 369 S.E.2d 624 (1988)

5. <u>State v. Fox</u>, 254 N.C. 97, 118 S.E.2d 58 (1961)

6. <u>Town of Benson v. County of Johnston</u>, 209 N.C. 751, 185 S.E. 6 (1936)

7. <u>Hunt v. Cooper</u>, 194 N.C. 265, 139 S.E. 446 (1927)

For Nos. 8–11, give the complete citation, including subsequent history, in accordance with *Bluebook* rules.

8. <u>Edmonds v. Fresenius Med. Care</u>, 165 N.C. App. 811, 600 S.E.2d 501 (2004)

9. <u>Watson v. Dixon</u>, 130 N.C. App. 47, 502 S.E.2d 15 (1998)

10. <u>Fulton Corp. v. Justus</u>, 338 N.C. 472, 450 S.E.2d 728 (1994)

11. <u>IRT Prop. Co. v. Papagayo, Inc.</u>, 112 N.C. App. 318, 435 S.E.2d 565 (1993)

Chapter 11

Computer-Assisted Legal Research

Nearly all authoritative legal resources are available in books. Today, more and more of those same sources can also be found online. But, for comprehensive research using a computer, the information available on the Web is insufficient: you need a good computer research service. Such services provide you with statutes, constitutions, cases, administrative rules, an array of secondary sources, forms, information from public records, and more, as well as an effective means for searching them.

Books versus Computer

With so much now available on the computer, why go to the books? The utility of a computer for research is incontrovertible. However, the extent to which you use one depends upon many factors, including access, cost, and the nature of your project. Even "free" government websites require a computer with internet access and may offer only limited information. Without books, you need a high quality computer-assisted legal research service for a complete set of legal materials. Such services cost money, and many law firms and legal departments do not subscribe to one.

On the other hand, computer assisted legal research services have the advantage of having everything in one place, accessible via the internet from your home or office, and updated on a daily basis. New decisions may be available within hours of being handed down by the court. *Shepardizing* or otherwise validating your research doesn't require a multitude of supplements: the service handles all that for you and provides you with extremely current information.

When you research an area of the law using a computer, the process may be somewhat different than in books. Books are typically indexed with descriptive words and phrases to help you find a specific topic. These words and phrases may or may not be contained within the actual text of the authority, but get you to the right subject area. For example, when you search for cases dealing with automobile racetracks as nuisances, you might look up "nuisance" in the index to a digest. Within the topic of "nuisance," you might look for a sub-topic such as "racetrack."

The digest will provide you with cases concerning a racetrack or speedway as a nuisance.

When searching via computer for the same cases, you may not find a traditional index. Instead, you will ask the computer to search a particular database for specific words you believe are likely to be contained in the case, statute, or other resource you are seeking. For example, when researching an automobile racetrack case, you might tell the computer to search for cases containing the word "nuisance." It will provide you with every case in the database you searched that includes that word, conceivably hundreds, or even thousands, of cases, depending upon the database you used.

You might narrow your search to look specifically for racetrack nuisance cases by asking the computer to search for cases including the words "nuisance" and "racetrack" in the same opinion. However, the computer will not give you any cases where the case uses the word "speedway" instead of "racetrack." Nor will it give you cases where "ractrack" is spelled as two words, i.e. "race track." And, it will give you cases that included the words "racetrack" and "nuisance" even if the case was about something else. For example, it could turn up nuisance cases involving track and field events; or even a case where an inebriated fan made a "nuisance" of himself at a horse race.

Of course, there are methods for refining your search so that you can access only the kinds of cases you want, for example, by asking the computer to find cases containing the words "automobile," "nuisance" and either "racetrack" or "speedway." Just keep in mind that the cases the computer finds will be based upon the actual search words you use, not the overall subject matter of those words.

Computer-Assisted Legal Research Services

There are two primary services now in use in North Carolina for conducting computer-assisted legal research: Lexis and Westlaw. A legal office may not have access to both services. However, they operate in similar ways. Once you are familiar with one service, you can easily translate your skills to the other.

Lexis and Westlaw both offer comprehensive materials. However, subscribers may economize by paying for packages that include less than the entire Lexis or Westlaw database. For example, a North Carolina law office that specializes in state law issues might pay a lower fee and receive primarily North Carolina materials. Another office might also want other state materials, while a third office might buy only federal sources. Both Lexis and Westlaw tailor their offerings to suit the needs of the particular law firm or company. Thus, the materials you can access may be limited by the level of service your law office has requested.

If your office subscribes to a full array of material, you can find virtually any type of resource you need on either service, including primary and secondary authorities. You will find on Lexis an emphasis on those secondary authorities that it publishes in book form, and on Westlaw, an emphasis on those published by West. Since most researchers are more interested in primary authorities, the distinction between the two may not be terribly important. Primary authorities are the same on both services. The extra features that come with the primary authorities vary (annotations, editors' notes and the like), just as they do in book form.

Of course, someone must pay for the research you do on either service. Fees typically are charged based upon the number of minutes you spend connected to the service or the number of "transactions" you have with the service, depending upon how your office chooses to be billed. Some large offices negotiate a flat rate contract for unlimited use (based upon that office's average use). In general, however, you must be careful to be as efficient as possible. Even if fees are passed on to the client, the costs for computer-assisted legal research will be carefully scrutinized.

Lexis and Westlaw continually update their databases, and the means of providing information to users. Thus, the information provided in this chapter may not be current by the time you read it here. Too, for maximum efficiency and results on a computer-assisted research service, you would be well-advised to take a hands-on training course and obtain an instruction manual for the particular service you use. These are typically provided by the service, along with up-to-date information on its latest enhancements. Check the instructional materials online at www.Lexis.com or www.Westlaw.com, look for tutorials within the program, or contact your service representative for more information.

Lexis

To access the full Lexis database, you will need a computer with internet access, and a Lexis identification number and password. Once you have these, go to www.Lexis.com, enter your i.d. number and password in the boxes provided, and click "sign on."

After you sign on, you will be presented with a screen that mimics index cards with five tabs running across the top: *Search, Research Tasks, Search Advisor, Get a Document*, and *Shepard's®*.

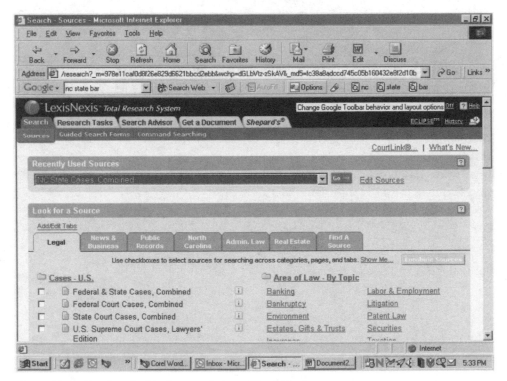

Figure 11.1   Reprinted with the permission of LexisNexis.

Get a Document

If you know exactly what you need, the easiest and quickest way to get it is by clicking the *Get a Document* tab. You can get the document by using a citation, party name, or docket number. Click on the appropriate tab, type in the information you have, and hit "Enter."

If you are getting the document by citation, you don't have to enter the it in *Bluebook* form to make it work. For example, if you need a copy of *Renwick v. News and Observer*, 310 N.C. 312, 312 S.E.2d 405 (1984), you can simply enter "310 NC

312"or "312 SE2d 405" in the box (without periods) and click "get" or hit "Enter." Or, if you are looking for Title 18 of the U.S. Code, Section 1, type, "18 USC 1." Lexis accepts a variety of formats for your citations. For example, when searching for a North Carolina statute, it will accept, "NCGS," N.C.G.S.," "N.C. Gen. Stat." and even "N.C. Stat." Typically, you can include or omit periods, no matter what you are seeking. If you are unsure of the citation format needed to pull up a particular resource, you can click on "Citation Formats" and an "assistant" will provide guidance.

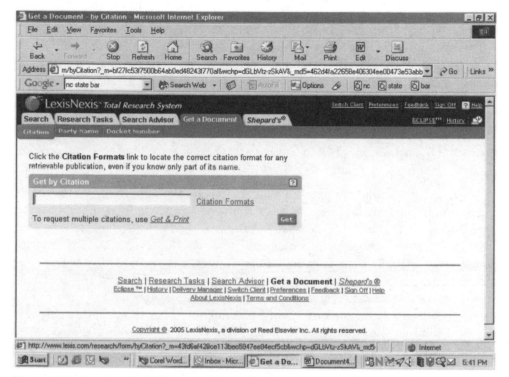

Figure 11.2   Reprinted with the permission of LexisNexis.

It is easiest to find a document by its citation. (See Figure 11.2.) If necessary, however, you may search for a case by clicking on the *Party Name* tab, and entering the information you have available. If a party name is too common, you will have difficulty finding the specific case you need using this technique. You can refine your search by adding a second party's name, and/or by scrolling down to add date restrictions.

Once you have entered sufficient information and hit "Enter," the document will appear on your screen. You can use *Get a Document* to pull up cases, statutes, administrative regulations and law review articles.

Search

If you don't have a citation already, and are looking for materials on a particular topic, then you need to conduct a search. Lexis typically will open to the "Search" page, but if not, click on the tab labeled *Search* at the top. Refer back to Figure 11.1 for a sample. Here, you will see two primary search options:

- *Recently Used Sources* and
- *Look for a Source* (including tabs for *Legal, News & Business, Public Records* and *Find a Source*. Additional tabs can be added for specific jurisdictions, like "North Carolina," and/or topics like "Administrative Law" or "Real Estate.")

After using Lexis for awhile, you may find that you routinely use the same twenty or fewer sources, and that you can conveniently get to them by clicking on the down carat [▼] under *Recently Used Sources*. Until then, for mainstream legal research materials, you will, "Look for a Source" under either the *Legal* or *Find a Source* tab. If you choose the *Legal* tab (typically the default setting) your choices will be laid out in front of you, including categories for *Cases—U.S., Federal Legal—U.S., State Legal—U.S.*, and *Legislation & Politics*. Within each category are subcategories to choose from.

Your decision about where to conduct your search is important. For example, again assume you are looking for cases about racetracks as legal nuisances. You probably won't find much under *News & Business*, or *Public Records*. Even within the *Legal* tab, you must decide how broad to make the search. Do you want to search all federal and state cases across the country, all state cases (no federal), or just all North Carolina cases? Look at the options and choose the one that best suits your purposes. Here again, money is an issue. It takes longer, and therefore costs more, to search a larger database. So, if you only need North Carolina cases, it is better to conduct your search in the *States Legal—U.S.* section, then click on *View Other States* to find North Carolina.

If you cannot find the source you want on the *Legal* page, you can instead click on the *Find a Source* tab and type the name of the source you are seeking in the box. Hit "Enter" or click *Find*. You will be provided a list of sources that match the words you typed. Until you learn the short-form names of sources used by Lexis, use the option for finding a source using the "long name."

Once you have chosen the source for your search, you must tell the computer what to look for. After clicking the source, you will see a box directing you to *Enter Search Terms*. There are two methods for constructing a search request: *Terms and Connectors*, and Natural Language.

Search Using Terms and Connectors

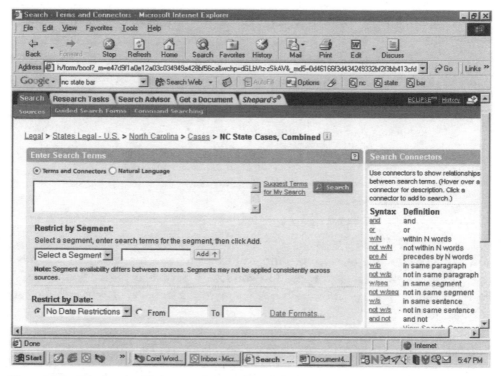

Figure 11.3   Reprinted with the permission of LexisNexis.

A *Terms and Connectors* search involves the use of codes, or symbols, to instruct the computer on the parameters of your search. To conduct such a search, click on the open circle in front of the phrase, "Terms and Connectors." Inside the open box, type in your search terms. In general, type them in the singular form, and Lexis will find plurals and possessives (e.g., "landlord" will pull up cases using the words, "landlord," landlords," "landlord's" or "landlords'.") However, Lexis cannot on its own figure out other forms of the word you are searching. For example, if you type in the word "negligence," Lexis will search for all cases containing that word. However, it will not pull cases including only the word "negligent."

To solve this problem, a *Terms and Connectors* search allows you to use "universal characters" so that the computer finds all forms of the word. For example, you can use an asterisk ("*") in place of any letter or other character. Thus, you could ask the computer to search for "negligen**," and it would find cases including the word "negligent" and "negligence." Similarly, you can put an exclamation point ("!") at the end of a word in place of an unlimited number of additional letters. For instance, entering "insura!" would find all cases including "insurance" or "insurable." (On the other hand, "ins!" would bring up not only cases including the words insurance or insurable, but also the words insert, inside, insist, insincere, and a host of others. You must therefore make your partial word long enough to exclude unde-sirable words.)

In addition to using the asterisk or exclamation point to broaden your search, you can enter various "connectors" to link search terms together. The most widely used connectors are:

or	finds one or both words, e.g., *"racetrack or speedway"*
and	finds two words in the same document, e.g. *"racetrack and nuisance"*
and not	excludes the identified word from the search, e.g., *"contractor and residen! and not commercial"*
/n	finds two words within a specified number of words from one another, e.g. *"automobile /5 racetrack"*
/s	finds two words within the same sentence, e.g., *"malpractice /s physician"*
/p	finds two words within the same paragraph, e.g., *"contract /p breach."*

You can also combine these connectors to further refine your search, as in, *"race-track or speedway and nuisance."* And, if you have a particular phrase you are seek-ing, you can simply type it in the box, e.g. *"false light invasion of privacy."* You can use the quotation marks, or not.

Search Using Natural Language

Some people find the "Terms and Connectors" method difficult or hard to re-member. Lexis offers an alternative search option using "natural language." This op-tion works more like a search in GOOGLE® or other internet search engines. Sim-ply type the words or phrase you are seeking, or even form your search as a question. Use parentheses to denote a synonym: "Has an automobile racetrack (speedway) been held a legal nuisance?" Lexis recommends a natural language search for complex or conceptual issues, and when you are uncertain what search terms to choose.

Help with Search Terms

If you need help coming up with search terms, you can click on "Suggest Words and Concepts for Entered Terms" and receive a list of alternatives or additions to those you have tried.

Restricting Your Search Using Segments

Once you have entered your search terms, Lexis allows you to further restrict your search using "segments," that is, specific parts of a document. For example, you can search only the main body of a court opinion and skip the dissent, or vice versa. You can search for cases decided by a particular court or judge, or for cases written in a particular time frame. These options will help you refine your search even more.

To search using segments, click on *Restrict Search Using Document Segments*. You will see a drop-down menu where you can choose the restrictions you want.

Search Advisor

At the top of the opening page is a tab labeled *Search Advisor* (right next to *Get a Document*). This feature allows you to search by topic, and obtain both primary and secondary authority about that topic, including cases, entries in treatises, law review articles, and news. It is best used when you know something about the area of law you are researching. It operates much like a table of contents: you choose a broad practice area of the law (e.g., torts) and then narrow your search within that area (e.g., nuisance) and then narrow it even further within that sub-topic, and so on, until you have reached the exact point of law you are seeking. Once there, you can click on the resource you would like to review (e.g., treatise or law review), or, you can enter search terms in the box presented to you to look for a particular word or phrase within the resources provided. You have the choice to search with terms and connectors, or natural language. Again, you can restrict your search by date or other segment.

Displaying Your Search Results

Once you have entered your search, the results of your search will come up on the screen. You can look at them a number of ways: "KWIC," "FULL," or "CITE." If you click on "KWIC," you will see your highlighted search terms in each of the results presented, including approximately 25 words on either side of it. This allows you to read your search terms in context to see if the results are good. If you click on "FULL," you will get the full text of each document. And, if you click on "CITE," you will see a numbered list of the citations for each result found. When you are in "KWIC" or "CITE," simply click on the authority you want to take you to the full text.

Shepardizing

Lexis now owns *Shepard's*, enabling its subscribers to Shepardize a case online. If you have already pulled up the case in question on Lexis, you can Shepardize it from there, or, you can click on the tab labeled "Shepard's" to Shepardize any case.

Assume you are searching for cases involving automobile racetracks as nuisances and have found references to several cases. When you pull up a particular case, at the top of the screen next to the case name, you will find a *Shepard's* icon. It may indicate positive or negative treatment, or simply that other cases have cited it. Click on the icon to Shepardize the case.

If you don't already have the case on your screen, you can go to the Lexis opening page and click on the tab labeled *Shepard's*. You will be prompted to enter a citation for the document you want to check. Enter a volume number, reporter abbreviation, and page number for the case, e.g., "276 NC 231." You do not have to include punctuation, such as periods, but you must include a space on either side of the abbreviated name of the reporter. Under the box for the case cite, you will be provided the option to obtain a *FULL* report or a *KWIC* report. Both include subsequent history and citing references that may affect the validity of your case. A *FULL* report also includes prior history, and additional citing references. Click on the circle for the option you prefer, then click on "✓Check" or hit "Enter."

The results will be the same as you would get from the *Shepard's* books, but will look much different on the screen. And, instead of having to look in reporters and other source books for information about each case in the history, and each citing authority, you can access these with a mouse-click.

As noted above, once you have the case pulled up that you want to Shepardize, you will see an icon at the top of the page, to the left of the case name (assuming there is at least one case or authority that mentions your case or is part of its history). The five possible signals are a red octagon (designed to look like a stop sign) indicating negative treatment, a yellow triangle indicating caution—possible negative treatment, a green diamond with a "+" inside, indicating positive treatment, a circle with an "A" inside indicating the case has been cited by others (neutral analysis), or a circle containing an "i" indicating simply that citing information is available.

Just because you see a red stop-sign beside your case, do not assume that it is no good for your purposes. You need to determine what sort of negative treatment the case received, and on what point of law. For example, it could be that a higher court criticized the case because of a procedural failing that has nothing to do with the substantive issue you are researching. You must look at the case history and negative treatment yourself to determine the validity of the case.

After the case name, you will see a *SHEPARD'S SUMMARY* outlining how many cases are in each of the five categories listed above (warning, caution, positive, neutral, other). You may click on any of these to see the relevant cases or other authorities in that category.

Next you will see citations to the "history" of your case, including prior history, and then subsequent history. The list will include your citation on a gray backdrop. Prior history will precede it on the page, subsequent history will come after. Thus, you can see where the case fits in its overall history through the courts.

Finally, just as in the books, you will see citing decisions and other citing authorities. These appear in order by jurisdiction, and within each jurisdiction, by date. For example, if you are Shepardizing a North Carolina case, in the citing authorities section you will first see North Carolina Supreme Court opinions that discuss your case. These will appear in chronological order with the most recent appearing first. Next will be N.C. Court of Appeals decisions, followed by U.S. Court of Appeals opinions (organized by circuit, with the 4th circuit appearing first), U.S. District Court opinions, and finally other authorities such as A.L.R.

Of course, you can click on any of the listings to read it in full. And, you can narrow your review of the listings by various means, including customizing your reports, clicking on any of the particular types of treatment in which you are interested, or using the *FOCUS®* feature to search within the listings displayed for particular points of law or fact.

Westlaw

To access Westlaw, you will need a computer with internet access, and a Westlaw password. Once you have these, go to www.westlaw.com, enter your password and sign on.

After you sign on, you will be presented with three choices: *Find this document by citation, KeyCite this citation*, and *Search these databases*. These are comparable to the Lexis options, *Get a Document, Shepardize* and *Search*.

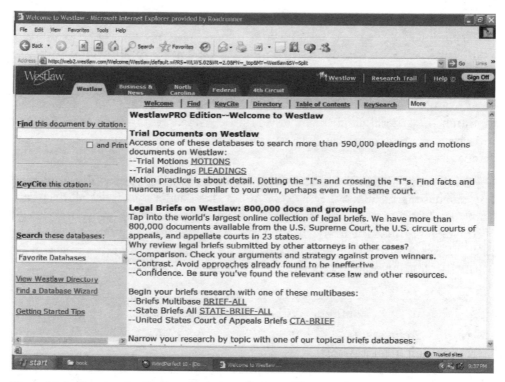

Figure 11.4   Reprinted with the permission of West, a Thomson business.

Find This Document by Citation

If you know exactly what you need and you have a citation, use *Find this document by citation*. Enter the citation in the template provided, hit "Enter," and Westlaw will pull it up for you, whether case, statute, or rule. Like Lexis, punctuation and capitalization are generally unnecessary, and you can use upper or lower case letters.

When searching for cases, you may enter the citation of any reported version, including the official reporter, unofficial reporter, or a looseleaf service. When searching for statutes, use a two-letter state abbreviation (typically the state's postal code), followed by a hyphen and "ST," and then the section number, e.g., "NC-ST58-36-1." This means you don't have to know the name of the code in any given state — you can simply enter the state's two-letter postal code, the abbreviation "ST," and the statute number to get right to the section you need.

Westlaw's *Find a Document* feature also works for secondary authorities, like law reviews and treatises. For assistance with particular publications in which to look, click on the *Find* link on the top of any Westlaw page. Click on the link to a comprehensive *Publications List*. This is similar to Lexis's *Citation Formats*. Or, click on "Find a Database," and a "wizard" will help you.

Search

If you don't have a citation, you can search in Westlaw much as you would in Lexis. You must first determine where you want the computer to search. Westlaw includes a vast array of databases. You will save time and money, and have more useful results, if you choose the right one to start. For instance, if you are interested in only North Carolina cases on defamation of character, there is no need to search the federal database or other states' databases. On the other hand, if your issue centers around a federal issue, you would be better off in a federal database.

Each Westlaw database carries its own identifier. For example, North Carolina's case database is identified as, "NC-CS-ALL." This database includes all decisions from the North Carolina courts, and all federal decisions where the court has applied North Carolina law to the dispute between the parties. If you do not need any federal cases, you can use a smaller database, "NC-CS," to limit your search to North Carolina appellate decisions only.

Common Westlaw Database Identifiers	
North Carolina cases w/federal	NC-CS-All
North Carolina cases only	NC-CS
All federal cases	ALLFEDS
All federal and state cases	ALLCASES
United States Supreme Court	SCT
United States Court of Appeals, 4th Circuit	CTA4
United States District Courts for NC	DCTNC
North Carolina statutes	NC-ST or NC-ST-ANN
United States Code	USC
United States Code Annotated	USCA

If you do not know the database identifier, you can click on "Westlaw Directory" for a list of choices.

Search Using Terms and Connectors

Once you have chosen the database, enter it in the box and hit the "Enter" key on your keyboard. Now you must formulate a search "query." You can use *Terms and Connectors*, or *Natural Language*. As in Lexis, a search with terms and connectors involves the use of a sort of code to tell the computer what to look for.

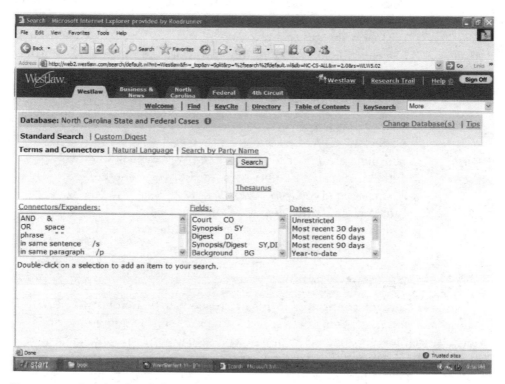

Figure 11.5   Reprinted with the permission of West, a Thomson business.

To conduct a search using connectors, click on the phrase "Terms and Connectors" if it is not already highlighted. Then, inside the open box, type in your search terms. If you type them in singular form, Westlaw will pull up documents including plural and possessive forms of the word also. However, remember that Westlaw will not pull up synonyms for your search terms: if you type in the word "corporation" as a search term, it will ignore any cases including only the word "company."

When searching Westlaw using *Terms and Connectors*, you may use the same universal symbols as in Lexis. The asterisk substitutes for any one letter or character anywhere in the word ("c*t" searches for "cat," "cot," and "cut" while "co*" searches for "cob," "cod," "cog," "con," "cop," etc.). The exclamation point searches for multiple letters or characters, and is used at the end of a word. For example, "defam!" will bring up cases including the word, "defame," "defamatory," and "defamation."

You also can use various connectors to link search terms together. Some typical Westlaw connectors are:

or	Rather than writing the word "or," the concept of "or" is represented by a single space and finds documents containing either or both words. For example, "*racetrack speedway*" will pull up documents containing the word "racetrack," the word "speedway," or both. However, Westlaw also recognizes the word "or" if you find it easier to use it. (But, when your search is reprinted, the "or" will be missing at the top of your results.)
and; &	Use either "and" or "&" to find two words in the same document, e.g. "*racetrack and nuisance*" or "*hous! & discriminat!*"
%	This symbol excludes the identified word from the search, e.g., "*negligen! % gross.*" If you cannot remember this symbol, you can instead simply type in the phrase, "but not" and Westlaw will pull up the same set of cases.
/n	Substitute a number for the "n", and Westlaw will find two words within a specified number of words from one another, e.g. "*automobile /5 racetrack*" asks Westlaw to search for the word "automobile" within five words of "racetrack."
/s	This connector finds two words within the same sentence, e.g., "*malpractice /s physician*"
/p	Similarly, the "/p" finds two words within the same paragraph, e.g., "*contract /p breach.*"

You can also combine connectors to further refine your search, as in, "*racetrack speedway and nuisance.*" And, you can include a phrase inside quotation marks, in order to search for any document containing just that phrase, as in, "*public policy exception.*" However, unlike Lexis, you cannot omit the quotation marks. If you do, Westlaw will interpret your spaces as "or" and will look for "public or policy or exception."

Search Using Natural Language

Westlaw also offers an alternative search option using "natural language." A natural language search may be easier to formulate, especially when you are new to Westlaw or when you are uncertain what search terms to choose. Simply click on the "Natural Language" circle and type your question in the box, e.g., "*Does North Carolina recognize a public policy exception to the employment at will doctrine?*"

Restricting Your Search Using Segments

Westlaw also allows you to restrict your search by date, and to particular "fields." The options vary, depending upon whether you search using terms and connectors, or natural language. A search using terms and connectors gives you more options. Among others, you can limit your search to:

- just the titles of the documents in the database you have chosen,
- the opinions of a particular judge,
- the opinions from a particular court,
- the cases involving a particular attorney, or
- cases or documents in a particular time frame.

To limit your search to particular fields, click on the field within which you want to search and type your restriction within the parens. For example, if you are searching North Carolina District Court cases for those including the phrase "public policy," you could click on "Judge (JU)" under "Fields" and type "Smith" in the parens, to limit your search to cases including the phrase "public policy" that were decided by Judge Smith.

If you are searching using natural language, click on "Add Date Restrictions" or "Add Other Restrictions." The latter will allow you to limit your search to a particular court, attorney, or judge.

Displaying Your Search Results

Once you have entered your search terms, your results will be displayed on the screen, with the terms you entered highlighted in yellow and enough surrounding text to identify the context in which your terms appear. You can click on the title of any case you want to read in full. If you get too many (or too few) results to be useful, go to "Edit Search" at the top of the results.

Validating Your Research: KeyCite

Since Lexis (not West) now owns *Shepard's*, you cannot "Shepardize" per se on Westlaw. However, Westlaw has developed its own method to allow subscribers to validate their research, called "KeyCite." KeyCite uses a system of red and yellow flags, along with blue letters, to show you at a glance the status of your case. For example, if you have a case pulled up on your screen, you can check the color of the flag at the top of the page. A red flag denotes negative treatment or history; yellow means there is possible negative treatment and you should exercise caution. The color blue is neutral. A blue "H" means there is history for the case, and a "C" means there is treatment of the case, namely citing cases. Click on the icon to see the details. If there is no flag or letter, then there is no history or treatment of the case.

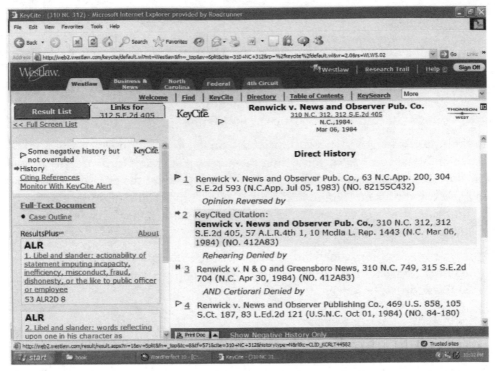

Figure 11.6   Reprinted with the permission of West, a Thomson business.

If you don't already have the case on your screen, go to the Westlaw opening page, enter your citation in the box labeled, "*KeyCite* this citation," and hit "Enter." If you are checking cases, you will be provided with any negative history of the case first, marked with a red flag. You can ask for the full history of the case by clicking *Show Full History* or limit the display to *Negative History Only*, by clicking the grey bar on the bottom. The full history will include the full citation of the case you are checking. And, if you want to review any of the citing references to the case you are checking, you can click on *Citing References* in the box on the left to see cases, law reviews and A.L.R. articles that discuss your case.

As noted, when you pull up a case using KeyCite, you will see its full history, but not the text of the opinion itself. On the other hand, if you pull up the same case using "Find," Westlaw will give you the full opinion, but only the most important KeyCite icon, e.g. a red or yellow flag. Remember, such a flag doesn't mean there isn't other history or treatment. To look at other citing cases, including negative treatment, you must go to a second screen, "History," or "Citing References" by clicking the appropriate link in the small box on the left.

Be sure to look at the cases that treat yours negatively. Until you read each decision, you cannot be sure of the reason for its negative treatment. You may find that it has nothing to do with point of law you are researching.

Internet Research

In addition to the computer-assisted legal research services like Lexis or Westlaw, there are many resources available online, and these are free. However, many of these are not easily searched, if you don't know exactly what you are looking for. When you use such resources, be sure to check the date the site was last updated so that you can determine how current the information is.

A good way to access a variety of resources is through a law library web page. For example, many law libraries' internet sites have excellent links to a variety of resources. Those for both the University of North Carolina ("UNC") and Duke are discussed below, but there are other good choices. Explore the websites of all five North Carolina law schools and use the one you find the most useful.

UNC Law Library

Go to http://library.law.unc.edu/ for the UNC law library page, and click on the appropriate link. Two especially useful links are *NC Legal Research* for North Carolina resources, and *Legal Research on the Web* for national resources. Under the *NC Legal Research* tab, you can access state statutes, state administrative materials including rules, recent state cases and cases from the 4th Circuit, various forms, and an array of other materials. Through the *Legal Research on the Web* option, you can access federal materials, including recent federal appellate cases and U.S. Supreme Court cases, also the C.F.R. and Federal Register, links to federal agencies, and links to resources from other states.

Duke Law Library

Similarly, the Duke website is equally useful. Go to http://www.law.duke.edu/lib/ and look under *Resources*. You will find a helpful table if you click on *Legal Research Sources*, including links to the same sorts of sites described above, and a number of others. Duke's site includes links to other sites that require a password for entry, including Lexis and Westlaw, and sites which require the user to be on a Duke computer network. However, there are a number of sites listed which require no special dispensation to enter. For example, there is a link in the table to *North Carolina Law* which brings up additional links to cases, statutes, state government sites, the Institute of Government, and the North Carolina State Bar. There are also a number of links to national resources.

Maintaining Your Own "Library"

Of course, once you have found a site you like, you may access it directly, without going through a library or other site to get there. Keep the ones you use most frequently in your "favorites" list on your computer. You will soon develop your own "library" of sorts, that efficiently takes you to the sites you need the most.

Exercise 11 — Lexis or Westlaw Exercises

1. Log on to Westlaw or Lexis. Using the *Get a Document* or *Find a Document* feature, pull up *Renwick v. News and Observer*, 310 N.C. 312, 312 S.E.2d 405 (1984).

2. Based upon the summary provided, briefly describe what the case is about.

3. Click on the icon to *Shepardize* (Lexis) or validate the case using *KeyCite* (Westlaw). List the subsequent history of the case.

4. How many citing cases are there?

5. Is the case still good law?

6. Go back to the home page and conduct a search using *Terms and Connectors* for a case in North Carolina involving fraud by an appraiser.
    A. Give your search terms just as you entered them in the *Terms and Connectors* box.

    B. How many hits did you get?

    C. Cite the first case listed in your results.

7. Now narrow your search for appraisal fraud cases by using the *Segment Searching* (Lexis) or *Field Restrictions* (Westlaw) feature. Look for cases that have been decided within the last 10 years.
    A. How many hits did you get?

    B. Cite the first case provided. If it is the same case as you cited in response to question 6(C) above, cite the next case provided instead.

    C. Pull up the case you cited in the answer above to Question 7(B).
        (1) Briefly summarize the facts of the case

        (2) Is the case good law?

(3) Give the case name for one example of any positive or negative treatment the case has received including the type of treatment (positive, negative, neutral) and the citation of the case giving it that treatment.

8. Go to the Carolina Law Library website and click on *NC Legal Research*.

   A. Find the link to the North Carolina General Statutes and go there. Give the website to which you are sent.

   B. Search the statutes for Chapter 93E of the N.C. General Statutes. What is the short title of the Act? (Name the short title and give the citation to the section where you found it.)

   C. Cite the last section in the chapter.

   D. Describe the penalties for violating the chapter and cite the section describing them.

9. Go back to the Carolina Law Library home page, *NC Legal Research*, and find your way to the North Carolina appellate cases.

   A. Give the web address where the NC Supreme Court and Court of Appeals opinions are located.

   B. Scroll down the page to determine from what date forward the cases are reported.

      NC Supreme Court:

      NC Court of Appeals:

   C. Using the function that allows you to search by keyword, do a search using terms and connectors to look for cases involving fraud by an appraiser.

      (1) Exactly what words did you enter?

      (2) Give the first case listed as it appears in the list.

      (3) Click on the first case listed. Do its facts involve an appraiser who committed fraud? If not, what is the case about?

10. Go to the Duke Law Library web page and click on *Legal Research Sources*.

A. Click on the link to federal law, and find the link to the official U.S. Code. Search for 15 U.S.C. 1. What is the statute about?

B. Search the U.S. Code for the "Patriot Act."

   (1) Does it take you to only one title of the Code?

   (2) Find an entry dealing with an "unusual and extraordinary threat" and click on it. Cite the title and section that appear.

C. Go back to the Duke Law Library page giving links to federal law sites. Find the U.S. Supreme Court.

   (1) Identify the website.

   (2) Search the site for a case involving an appraiser, and identify the parties in the first case listed.

Chapter 12

Organizing and Writing Up Your Research

Ultimately, the goal of most research projects is to report your results in written form. Sometimes this is as simple as copying or printing the relevant primary authorities and handing them in. More often, you must organize, analyze, and write up the results of your research.

Organizing Your Research

In order to write an orderly report of your findings, it helps to be organized from the beginning. Before you start a project, consider how you might best go about it. Can you go straight to a statute book and find the answer, or do you need some background information on the problem first? Develop a list of source materials that you believe will help you, and determine the order you want to look at them. In general, if you are researching an area of law that is new to you, it is helpful to begin with some secondary authorities.

As you work with each source, **take notes** about the kind of information it includes. Print or make copies of pertinent sections for your records so that you can refer back to them later. (When working on a pay-as-you-go computer research service, print the information you find and read it offline to save money.) If you might quote from the source, make sure you have the exact wording and punctuation, and the page number(s) on which the material appears. Brief important cases, or do mini briefs that include the important facts, legal issue, and holding.

In each source, look for any helpful cross-references to other sources and add the new ones to your list. Remember that each source you use has the potential to (1) provide you with substantive information, and (2) be a finding tool for other resources.

Keep track of where you've been. To avoid wasteful repetition, check off each source after you have completed searching it. Note the search terms that you tried, and whether they worked, or not. (If you don't, you may find yourself repeating searches you have already done—typically the ones that didn't work!) If using West products, note the key numbers and topics that were most helpful, and the ones that were not. You can use the good ones in other West sources.

When you finish each source, consider whether you might cite it in your final product. If there is any chance that you will, **take careful notes of all necessary information for your citation**, including volume and page numbers, year of decision or publication, authors, editors, publishers, and the like. There is nothing worse than discovering at the last minute that you cannot cite an authority because you didn't note all the necessary information. And, before you put away any book, be sure to **check the supplement** for the most current information on your topic.

When are you done? There are a number of clues. One is that you have finished looking at everything on your list, including those sources you added during the research process. Another is that every source you read points you to other sources you have already reviewed. Research can be a circular process; when what you are doing keeps bringing you back around to where you have already been, it's a sign you have found what there is. A final clue that you are done relates to time. Usually, you will have only a limited time to complete your research. Plan to finish with the research in time to organize what you have found, compose a well-written presentation, and submit it before the deadline.

Research Tips and Shortcuts

There are many ways to research a topic. When you are on a tight deadline, remember the following shortcuts.

Hornbooks and Law Student Study Aids

Hornbooks and law student study aids are excellent background resources. They will provide you with an easy-to-read summary of the topic, and references to other sources of information. Most hornbooks and study aids are written to a national audience, and therefore include references to materials from across the country.

West Key Numbers

If you are using West products, once you have an applicable topic and key number, you can use it to cross reference other West publications on that specific point of law. Key numbers are most often used to find similar cases in other jurisdictions.

Shepard's

Shepardize cases, statutes, or regulations to find others that cite it. Although many people think of using *Shepard's* only to determine whether a case is good law, it can also be used to find other cases on the same topic. Find a headnote number you like in the case and look at the matching superscript numbers in the cases cited in *Shepard's* to find other cases on that same topic. *Shepard's* is also a good source for references to periodicals and A.L.R. articles.

A.L.R.

If you find a good *A.L.R.* article on your topic, a vast amount of your research will have been done for you. *A.L.R.* compiles information about the majority of states' view on an issue, the minority point of view, references to cases from many states, and references to other authorities. *A.L.R.* can be a gold mine of information. Don't forget to check the supplement of the volume you are using for updated information. Sometimes the articles are fairly old, but the supplement should be quite current.

Writing Up Your Results

How you write up your results depends upon the type of document you will prepare. You may be asked to create a "Memorandum of Law" in which you set forth an objective review of the facts and the law, or to write a "brief" in which you make a formal argument to the court about the merits of your client's case.

Writing a Memorandum of Law

The *Memorandum of Law*, or "memo" is a common form for writing up your research. Admittedly, it is more often a school exercise than a typical assignment in a law office, but the exercise will help you better understand the process of determining the strengths and weaknesses of a case.

You may be asked to write a memorandum to address how the law might be applied to a particular set of facts, often concerning a legal problem faced by a client, or prospective client, of your office. Your memo will be an internal document, designed to be read by those with whom you work. As such, it should be an objective review of the law on the subject.

Do not be tempted to take your client's side. The best service you and your legal office can give at this point is objectivity. Find the cases and other authorities that are most on point, and apply them to the case to determine the likely outcome.

Format

As with all writing assignments, the format of your memo will be dictated by those for whom you work. However, there are common elements in most legal memos. These include the:

- heading
- issue(s) and answer(s)

- facts
- analysis, including counter-analysis
- conclusion.

Depending upon the length and complexity of the memo, you may also include other sections, such as a:

- statement of assignment
- table of contents
- table of authorities
- summary
- recommendations.

Heading

The heading of your memo will typically identify the person to whom it is addressed, the author of the memo, a reference to the case or client to which it pertains, and the date. It may also include a brief reference to the topic addressed.

Sample Memo Heading

TO:	Mary Boyd, Legal Counsel
FROM:	Caroline Abbott
CASE NO.	05-1234; <u>Suarez v. ABC Incorporated and James Alpha</u>
RE:	Breaking & Entering; Intentional Infliction of Emotional Distress
DATE:	January 15, 2005

Statement of Assignment

In some cases, it is helpful to put a *Statement of Assignment* near the front of your memo. This is especially true if your research is to be limited in some way. Perhaps you are only to address a particular aspect of the case, leaving other issues to other people. Or, maybe you are to use only a limited number of resources. If your memo includes any such limitations, outline the task assigned to you and limitations imposed.

Issue

Your issue should be crafted much like an issue in a case brief. Thus, it should include the most important facts as well as the legal question presented. Think of the issue as consisting of two parts: a reference to the rule of law being applied in the case, whether from a statute, common law doctrine or elsewhere; and, a statement of the essential facts of the case that raise the legal issue at hand.

It is especially important to include facts in your issue when the issue comes ahead of the *Facts* section in your memo. If you simply ask a legal question, your reader will not understand the context of your memo. For example, in a case where a bouncer has used physical force to eject a rowdy patron, the issue might be framed as follows: "Is a nightclub liable in tort to a drunk and disorderly patron who was injured when the club's bouncer ejected him?" Note that the issue includes both law, and facts, and that by reading it you have an overview of the matter at hand. What are the essential facts of the case? A patron at a nightclub was drunk and disorderly. The bouncer used force to make him leave. What is the legal question presented? The question is whether the nightclub is responsible for the bouncer's conduct under tort law.

What if you omitted the facts from the issue? Then it might read, "Is a nightclub liable for torts?" In a broad sense, this is the question, but it is incomplete. It does not tell your reader anything about what happened. And, it presents a question with an answer that is so obvious it is completely unhelpful. Of course a nightclub can be liable for torts. The question is, under what circumstances? That requires the infusion of facts.

Practice Set 12.1

Assume that you are representing a wife in a divorce case. She has acted as the part-time bookkeeper for her husband's small business for the past seventeen years. She has never been paid a salary for these services, rather, she and her husband have lived off the profits of the business. However, the business is in her husband's name. North Carolina law provides for an "equitable distribution" of the assets of the marriage. You have been asked to write a memo outlining the wife's rights, if any to the future profits of the business upon their divorce. Try to frame an issue for your memo:

_____   _____

_____   _____

_____   _____

Sometimes your memo will involve more than one issue. If so, simply number each one and separate them with spaces. Try to put them in a logical order.

Example: Issues Section — Multiple Issues

Issue (1) Is a landlord guilty of "breaking and entering" under North Carolina criminal law if he forcibly enters his own residential rental property despite the protests of an existing tenant who is inside?

Issue (2) Is a landlord civilly liable to a tenant for intentional infliction of emotional distress if he forcibly enters his own residential rental property despite the protests of an existing tenant who is inside?

Answers to Issues

You may be asked to give a brief answer to each of your issues at the beginning of your memo. The answer might be as simple as "yes" or "no." Or, you might be asked to restate your issue as an answer: "Yes, a property owner is liable to a real estate agent for unilaterally canceling a listing contract prior to its termination date." If you are asked to add more detail, briefly add an explanation of why your answer is so: "Yes, a property owner is liable to a real estate agent for unilaterally canceling a listing contract prior to its termination date because the contract does not permit either party to cancel early."

If you have multiple issues, you may give the answer to the first issue before moving on to the next one. Alternatively, you may have two sections: *Issues* and *Answers*. In that case, set out each of your numbered issues in the first section, and then answer them in the second. If your answers are separated from the issues, it is best to restate the answer rather than writing only "yes" or "no."

Facts

The *Facts* section outlines the important facts of the case. It should be a chronological narrative of the events leading up to the dispute at hand. In general, start at the beginning and describe what happened. Tell the story as if you were describing the events to someone who knows nothing of the case. If it takes time to get to the point, consider starting with a one or two sentence summary describing what the case is about, followed by a full narrative of the events.

Write the *Facts* using the past tense. Don't say, "The landlord goes to the house at 5:30 in the morning and forces open the door, even though the tenant is yelling at him that he should leave." Instead say, "The landlord went to the house at 5:30 in the morning and forced open the door, despite the tenant's protests."

You may find that you do not know all the facts, or that some facts are in dispute. If you think a missing fact is important, note it. For example, you might write, "We do not know whether the landlord first rang the doorbell or otherwise announced his presence." If instead the fact is in dispute, you might say, "The landlord claims that he first rang the doorbell, and then shouted "hello" as he was entering the house to alert the tenant he was there. The tenant denies this." And, if you are uncertain that a "fact" is really true, add the basis for it. For example, write, "The tenant says that the landlord never rang the bell."

Your facts should be as objective as possible. Do not be tempted to slant the facts in favor of one party or the other. Try to use neutral words to describe what happened, rather than inflammatory or argumentative ones. For example, don't say, "The landlord maliciously forced open the door as the tenant heroically stood her ground." Instead, say, "The landlord pushed open the door, despite the tenant's efforts to keep it closed."

As you complete your memo, go back and reread the *Facts* section. Did you include information in your analysis that is not set out in the *Facts*? If something that happened was important enough to address in your analysis, then you should add it to the *Facts*. Are there facts laid out in the *Facts* section that were unimportant in your analysis of the case? If they are not necessary for understanding the events that occurred, consider omitting them.

Unless the matter is extremely complex, at the conclusion of your *Facts* section, you should be no more than one and a half or two pages into your memo, typed and single-spaced.

Although the *Facts* section is discussed here after the *Issue* section, you may be asked to reverse their order, much like a case brief. If you are given the choice, order the *Facts* and *Issue(s)* in the way that reads the best to you.

Analysis

Here, analyze the statutes, cases, and other authorities related to your issues. Your goal is to determine, as best you can, the likely outcome of your client's case. This section is the heart of your memo and typically the hardest to write. You must look at how the applicable authorities help and hurt your client, and remain as objective as possible.

If you have more than one issue, divide your analysis into sections, one for each issue. Give each section a heading. For example, if you are writing a memo about the landlord who forcibly entered his own house while it was occupied by a tenant, you might use the following two headings: (1) Criminal Liability—Breaking and Entering; and (2) Civil Liability—Intentional Infliction of Emotional Distress.

Unless your issues immediately precede the analysis, begin each section with a recap of the issue at hand. It need not be as thorough as in your *Issues* section. Rather, write a sentence that serves to focus your reader's attention on the topic you intend to address. For example, you might start your analysis with, "The first issue concerns the criminal liability of Mr. Landlord for entering his tenant's house by force."

Next, state the general rule of law that applies to the issue. This should encompass the elements of the cause action, e.g., breaking and entering, or intentional infliction of emotional distress. In theory, you will have learned the general rule from your research. In some cases, it may be obvious, as where a statute sets out the parameters of what is required or prohibited. For instance, there may be a statute that sets out the elements of "breaking and entering." If so, you may summarize it or quote it. Include a *Bluebook* style citation immediately afterward.

Example: Setting Out the General Rule of Law Using a Statute

North Carolina law provides that a person is guilty of misdemeanor "breaking and entering" when:

1. the defendant wrongfully breaks into;
2. or wrongfully enters;
3. any building, including dwellings, uninhabited houses, buildings under construction and other structures designed to house or secure within it any activity or property.

N.C. Gen. Stat. § 14-54 (2003).

At times, the rule of law won't be so obvious. There may not be a statute that tells you how a particular situation is handled. In such circumstances, look to the cases to determine the general rule for handling a particular kind of dispute. Often, the court opinions will lay out the elements necessary to make a particular kind of claim, or at least the manner in which the issue should be analyzed. Quote or summarize a court opinion that gives the general rule. Or, distill a general rule of your own based upon all the material you have read. Be sure to cite your source or sources for the rule in *Bluebook* form. Even if the rule is one you have distilled on your own, you must tell your reader the authorities on which you base your statement.

Example: Setting Out the General Rule Using Case Law

In order to be liable for intentional infliction of emotional distress in North Carolina, the court must find that the defendant:

1. engaged in extreme and outrageous conduct;
2. intended to cause and actually caused distress; and
3. the distress was severe.

Dickens v. Puryear, 302 N.C. 437, 452, 276 S.E.2d 325, 335 (1981).

Next, set out the most important cases and other authorities that address your issue one by one and apply them to the facts of your case.

Concentrate on primary authorities. Although you may have used several secondary sources to help you learn about the issue and the law, your memo should rely on the primary authorities. As precedents, they are mandatory, and therefore far more persuasive than secondary authority. Typically, most of your analysis will concentrate on cases.

In choosing which cases to address in your memo, you should consider several factors. First, look for cases that have similar facts to your client's situation or the fact pattern you have been given. If your case is about a child who is bitten by a pet dog, a case about a child bitten by a wild goose would be ineffective. The case could be better if it was about a wild dog. It probably would be better still if it was about a domestic cat. Best of all would be another case about a child bitten by a pet dog.

Also, choose cases where the issues are similar to yours. Suppose your case concerns a child who was bitten by a dog after she pulled a dog's tail; the child's parents want to know if the dog's owner is liable for the damages caused by the bite. If you find a dog-bite case where the issue is whether the authorities can put down an animal that bites someone, this case won't help you determine the question of the owner's liability to the injured party. Keep looking for better cases where the issues are similar to yours.

Address "leading cases," i.e. cases that are cited again and again by courts about a particular issue. They are often mentioned as having settled the question before the court for similar future disputes. Even if the case is old, if it is a leading case, it is worth discussing.

Also consider the age of the decision and the deciding court. In general, more recent cases are better than older cases, unless the older case is a leading one (see above). And, an opinion from a higher court carries more weight than an opinion from a lower court.

If you have to move outside your jurisdiction, look for cases from jurisdictions that will be looked upon favorably. For example, North Carolina courts are more likely to favorably consider cases from the surrounding states than opinions from a western, mid-western, or northern state. However, the courts of New York are generally well respected across the country, and the courts of California are often considered "leading-edge."

Once you have chosen the cases you will address, begin with the best cases you have in light of the considerations outlined above. Describe the facts of the case, and the court's holding. Cite the case in *Bluebook* form. Then, compare and contrast the facts of that case to the current dispute. How are the cases similar? How are they different? Would a court in our case likely rule the same way as it did in the case you are discussing?

Example: Case Analysis

In *State v. Branch*, 162 N.C. App. 707, 591 S.E.2d 923 (2004), Mr. Branch was stopped at a license and registration checkpoint. The officer conducting the check became suspicious of Mr. Branch when he produced a duplicate license, and because of the officer's familiarity with Mr. Branch from past interactions. He therefore called over a K-9 officer, whose dog detected the presence of narcotics. The officers then searched the car and found drugs. The court held that held that although the license check was constitutional, the use of the dog to sniff drugs was not. This case is similar to ours in that both Mr. Alpha and the Defendant Branch.... However, in the *State v. Branch* case,.... Applying *State v. Branch* to our case the likely result would be....

Move to the next case, and proceed in a similar manner. Be sure to outline the facts of each case you address. Do not make the mistake of simply summarizing points of law from the cases, or your memo will be far less effective.

You may have some cases that are somewhat like your client's but carry important differences. You can still address these cases in your memo. Point out the critical differences between the cases, and state whether these differences are such that the court might rule differently in the case before you.

Be sure to look at cases with opposing points of view. This part of the memo is sometimes referred to as "counter-analysis." For example, if the cases you have described to this point are all good for your client's position, bring up those that might not bode as well for him or her. You might start your paragraph of counter-analysis with, "On the other hand...." Compare and contrast the unfavorable cases to your client's dispute, and describe how they are the same, and different. Point out how these cases could indicate a possible bad result for your client. If the facts or issues of these cases are sufficiently different so that you do not expect they will hurt your client's position, explain how they can be "distinguished" from the client's case.

As you compare and contrast cases to your client's fact pattern, sum up your assessment of them. What will be the effect of the case or group of cases, on your client's situation? Even if you don't make a conclusion about each case as you discuss it, you should at least conclude at the end of your discussion of each issue how the court is likely to rule, before moving on to the next issue.

If you have more than one issue, begin your analysis of the second issue just as you began the first, by setting out the general rule addressing the next issue. As before, this might be a statute, or it might be the elements of a cause of action as distilled from case law. Then compare and contrast your client's case with the law and facts of each case you choose to address. Make conclusions as you go, considering cases on both sides of the issue, and making a final assessment of how this issue will turn out before moving to the next.

Conclusion

Once you have analyzed each issue, summarize your analysis with an overall conclusion. Here, you will simply reinforce the conclusions you have reached on each issue. You should not raise any new cases, statutes, or other authorities in this part of the memo. If they are important enough to address, they should be in the *Analysis* section. Essentially, you will briefly predict how a court is likely to rule on each issue presented. The *Conclusion* will therefore be short—probably only a paragraph.

Recommendations

You may find as you write that there is information you need that is unavailable to you. Perhaps you need additional facts beyond those provided, or access to a legal resource that you could not get. If this is so, add a *Recommendations* section to your memo outlining the information that needs to be obtained.

Table of Contents and Table of Authorities

If your memo is quite long, it may be helpful to add a *Table of Contents* and/or a *Table of Authorities* at the beginning of the memo. A *Table of Contents* will typically list each section of the memo and the page on which that section begins. Obviously, if your memo addresses one issue and is only a few pages long, a *Table of Contents* would be excessive. However, if the memo addresses a number of issues and is lengthy, you may want one. A *Table of Authorities* lists each of the authorities cited in the memo, in *Bluebook* form, and the page number(s) on which each authority appears. Again, this is useful for longer memos.

Style

Effective writing requires attention to style. How you organize your memo, set off quotations, and cite authorities affect your memo's readability and persuasiveness. Grammar, punctuation, and spelling are important. To improve your final product:

- Organize your memo in a clear, readable, fashion. Follow the format described above to give your memo a good overall structure. Within each section, consider how to most logically present your material. For example, in the *Facts* section, it is usually best to describe the facts in chronological order. In the *Analysis* section, you might start with the cases where the facts are most like yours. Or, you might consider first the "leading" cases, that is, the cases which the courts have repeatedly looked to concerning the issue at hand, and then move to more factually similar cases. Or, you could start with cases from the highest court and work down to the others.

- Be objective. Remember that a memo is not an argument, but rather an objective analysis of the merits of your client's position. If your client's position is bad, say so.

- Remember to analogize the facts of important cases to the client's facts. Don't just repeat statements of law from case after case. It is boring and not helpful to the reader's understanding of the issues.

- When quoting lengthy passages, i.e., those of fifty or more words, block indent. In other words, bring in both the left and right margins when you start your quote, and do not use quotation marks. For example, the following is a block-indented quote from *The Bluebook*:

  > **Quotations of forty-nine or fewer words** should be enclosed in quotation marks but not otherwise set off from the rest of the text. Quotation marks around material quoted inside another quote should appear as single marks within the quotation in keeping with the standard convention. The footnote number or citation should follow immediately after the closing quotation mark unless it is more convenient to place it elsewhere shortly before or after the quotation. Always place commas and periods inside the quotation marks; place other punctuation marks inside the quotation marks only if they are part of the matter quoted. When the material quoted would commonly be set off from the text, such as lines of poetry or dialogue from a play, the quotation may appear as a block quote per **rule 5.1(a)**, regardless of its length.[1]

- Cite an authority for each assertion you make about what the law is or requires. Use *Bluebook* form unless instructed otherwise.

- Don't string together more than two or three authorities in support of any particular point. String citing is distracting to the reader and takes up space. Pick the best authorities in support of your assertion and cite only those.

- Use short form citations for authorities you have already cited in accordance with *Bluebook* rules.

  » In general, after you have cited a statute once, you then can omit dates.

  » For cases, you can use the term, "*Id.*" in place of the case name for the case you just cited. You should still provide page numbers for the cited material, e.g., *Id.* at 22. If the citation to a case includes a parallel cite, you must give more information, e.g., *Id.* at 22, 333 S.E.2d at 444.

  » If you are referring to a case that you have cited before, but it is not the last one you cited, refer to it by a shortened version of the name that still identifies the one you mean. For example, having cited *United States v. Calandra*, 414 U.S. 338 (1974), you could then refer to it simply as *Calandra*, (not "*United States*" as there are too many cases with that name). If you are citing a particular page, then write, "*Calandra*, 414 U.S. at 343."

---

1. *The Bluebook: A Uniform System of Citation* R.5.1(b), at 44–45 (Columbia Law Review Ass'n et al. eds., 17th ed. 2000).

» Technically, you should not use the term "*supra.*" to refer to a case previously cited. However, many practitioners do. Be guided by applicable court rules and your supervisor's wishes.

- Pay attention to your spelling and grammar. Your substantive points will be lost if your reader is distracted by incomplete or run-on sentences, and misspelled and misused words. You are a professional and you must be able to express yourself orally and in writing.

- Avoid legalese. Words like "hereinafter" or "aforesaid" are boring and cause your reader to quit paying attention. Instead, use plain and direct language. Don't try to adopt words or grandiose phrases you wouldn't use in ordinary conversation. The end result is usually a sentence that doesn't read well and may make no sense.

Writing a Brief

Briefs are written arguments to a court on behalf of a party to a lawsuit. They may be directed to the trial court or an appellate court. Briefs to trial courts are typically in support of a motion, for example, a motion to dismiss the case or to require the other side to produce evidence. Briefs to appellate courts address whether the trial court conducted the proceedings correctly and whether the outcome of the case was supported by the evidence.

The objective of a brief is to convince the court that your client's position is correct. While you must remain truthful and accurate, you will write it in the light most favorable to your client, from the description of the facts to the analysis of the law.

Format

The format of a brief is often prescribed by the court to which it is directed. However, most trial court briefs include the following elements:

- caption
- statement of the case
- statement of the facts
- argument
- conclusion
- identification of counsel
- certificate of service.

If you are assisting in the preparation of any brief, be certain to check the rules of the court that will receive the brief to be sure it is in the right format and includes all the necessary information. Otherwise, the court could refuse to consider the matters contained in it.

For example, the North Carolina appellate courts have detailed requirements for briefs. These are set out in the North Carolina Rules of Appellate Procedure. Rule 28 lays out the specific requirements, which include all of the elements listed above, and also a:

- cover page
- subject index
- table of authorities
- statement of the questions presented.

In certain cases, an appellate brief requires an appendix including portions of the trial transcript relevant to the questions presented in the brief. It may also be that, in the *Argument* section, you will need an introductory argument on the "Standard of Review." In this section, you will describe the standard the appellate court must use to determine who wins and who loses.

Should you be required to assist in the preparation of an appellate brief, pay strict attention to the requirements of Rule 28 of the Rules of Appellate Procedure, and all the other rules it cross-references. Note that the rules specify not only the brief's format, but also the paper size and type, line spacing, lines per page, line width, and total pages, among other things.[2]

Caption

A typical brief includes the case caption identifying the parties, the court, the case number, and the document presented as set out in the box below.

North Carolina Wake County	In the General Court of Justice Superior Court Division Case No. 04 CVS 123456789

Jane S. Doe,   )
)
     Plaintiff)
)
    v.   )
)
Anne B. Carter and)
ABC Incorporated,)
)
     Defendants.)
	<u>Brief in Support of</u>
	<u>Defendants' Motion to Dismiss</u>

Statement of the Case

This section outlines the procedural history of a case, much like that in a case brief. Generally, you should describe the nature of the claims made, the court in which the case was filed, and a description of the case history. For example,

---

2. N.C. R. App. P. 26(g).

Plaintiff Jane S. Doe sued Defendants Anne B. Carter and ABC Incorporated in the Superior Court of Wake County on July 15, 2004, for breach of a real estate sales contract. Defendants filed an answer, including a motion to dismiss under Rule 12(b)(6) of the Rules of Civil Procedure, for failure to state a claim upon which relief can be granted....

Statement of the Facts

The Statement of the Facts includes all the facts pertinent to the questions presented for the court's consideration. These should be truthful and accurate, but you may summarize them in the light most favorable to your client(s). Start at the beginning and describe in chronological order what happened that resulted in the dispute between the parties. Use past tense: "Plaintiff and Defendant entered into a real estate contract in which the Plaintiff agreed to purchase the Defendants' property for $500,000.00" (not, "Plaintiff and Defendant enter into a real estate contract, in which the Plaintiff agrees to purchase the Defendants' property for $500,000.00").

The description of the facts often covers at least one full page, typed, double-spaced, and may take several pages to review in a complex case.

Argument

The argument is the main body of any brief. It is comparable to the *Analysis* section of a memorandum of law. In it, set forth the authorities that support your client's position, and analyze them. You must also address the authorities that hurt your position, and distinguish them from the case before the court.

Unlike the memo of law, a case brief is argumentative. Your goal is to persuade the court that your client's position is right. Use stronger language than in a memo, emphasizing the most favorable cases, statutes, and rules in support of your position. Although you may occasionally include a secondary authority, it is better to use primary authority if at all possible.

Follow the general format outlined in the *Analysis* section for the memo of law. As you address each case favorable to your client's position, focus on the similarity of facts and issues in the case to your client's case. Minimize the differences as much as possible, within the limits of truth and fairness. As you address cases that hurt your client's position, emphasize the facts and issues distinguishing them from those in the case before the court.

Remember that you must compare and contrast the facts and issues in most of the cases you cite with the facts and issues of the case before the court. Simply summarizing the main points of law in your cited cases will not be enough to convince a court of anything. You must **apply** the facts and law of the important cases to your case and show how the results in each one should affect the result in your case.

If there are several issues before the court, address each one in turn. Start with a strongly-worded heading describing the issue and the way you would like the court to resolve it. Such headings are usually written in all capital letters. For example, "PLAINTIFFS HAVE FAILED TO STATE A CLAIM FOR BREACH OF CONTRACT AND THEIR COMPLAINT SHOULD BE DISMISSED PURSUANT TO RULE 12(b)(6) OF THE RULES OF CIVIL PROCEDURE."

If you have more than one section in you argument, write a paragraph at the end of each section wrapping it up.

Conclusion

At the end of the *Argument*, include a separate paragraph labeled "Conclusion" in which you wrap up the reasons why your client should win. Your conclusion should highlight the main points of the argument. In general, avoid citing authority in the conclusion, and certainly don't include anything you haven't already addressed in the body of the argument itself.

Identification of Counsel

Courts typically require that the lawyers submitting a brief identify themselves by name, address, telephone number, and State Bar number. Courts typically require that briefs be dated and signed as well. The following is an example.

This the _____ day of _____, 200__.

_____

Miriam J. Baer
State Bar No. 123456789
Baer, Ray and Hernandez
Attorneys for the Defendants
1234 Elm Street
P.O. Box 5678
Raleigh, North Carolina 27602-5678
(919) 555-6789

Certificate of Service

Finally, the brief should include a certificate of the counsel submitting the brief that he or she has served it on the other party or parties to the case. In it, state how the brief was served, whether by mail, certified mail, hand-delivery, or otherwise.

Sample Certificate of Service

I, Miriam J. Baer, do hereby certify that I have this day served a copy of the attached *Appellant's Brief* on _____ [describe the party served] by depositing a copy of the same in the United States mail, postage prepaid, and addressed as follows:

_____

_____

_____

This the _____ day of _____, 200__.

_____

Miriam J. Baer
State Bar No. 123456789
Baer, Ray and Hernandez
Attorneys for the Defendants
1234 Elm Street
P.O. Box 5678
Raleigh, North Carolina 27602-5678
(919) 555-6789

Exercise 12 — Closed Memorandum of Law

{Date}

TO: _____

FROM: Attorney

RE: Memorandum of Law

FILE NO.   05-9876

Our clients are Raleigh Memorial Hospital and Dr. Meredith Welby.

Last September 10, Paul Perry, age nine, was playing on the school playground during recess. He had complained of stomach pains earlier in the day. While chasing after a ball, he fell and collapsed on the ground. A teacher determined that he was gravely ill, and called an ambulance and his mother, Jana Perry.

The ambulance rushed Paul to Raleigh Memorial Hospital where he was first treated in the emergency room. The emergency room staff determined that Paul was suffering from appendicitis and required immediate surgery to remove his appendix. Dr. Meredith Welby was the surgeon on call that day.

Dr. Welby met with Ms. Perry at the hospital and advised her of the urgent need for surgery. She told Ms. Perry that without surgery, Paul could die. Ms. Perry refused to give her consent for the surgery. She is a devoted member of a religion, one tenet of which provides that medical and health problems should be handled only with prayer. Ms. Perry told Dr. Welby, "God will cure my son."

Dr. Welby again urged Ms. Perry to reconsider, as Dr. Welby was convinced that Paul's appendix could burst at any time, and that he must have immediate surgery to guard against that happening. Ms. Perry continued to refuse her consent. Dr. Welby then consulted with the hospital administration and determined to proceed with the surgery without Ms. Perry's consent. She successfully performed an appendectomy and Paul recovered.

Ms. Perry has now threatened suit against Dr. Welby and Raleigh Memorial for operating on her son without her consent. Please write a 6–8 page memo outlining the law in this area, and discussing the liability of the hospital and Dr. Welby for performing the surgery. Concentrate on primary authority addressing this subject, including Constitutional provisions, statutes and cases (and administrative rules if any). Be sure to discuss the facts of the cases and compare and contrast them to the facts provided here. Use secondary authorities to help you find the law, and learn about the subject area. In general, avoid citing a secondary authority in your memo, unless that is the only source available.

Appendix

(Answers to the questions posed in the book)

Chapter 3

Practice Set 3.1

drive/driving; driving while impaired; driving under the influence; DUI; DWI

impaired; influence; drunk; intoxicated

alcohol/alocholic beverages; beer; wine; intoxicating liquor; liquor

vehicle; motor vehicle; car; automobile

penalty; punishment

crime; criminal law

Practice Set 3.2

Chapter 91A. Pawnbrokers Modernization Act of 1989.

§ 91A-1. Short title. This Chapter shall be known and may be cited as the Pawnbrokers Modernization Act of 1989. (1989, c. 638, s. 2.)

§ 91A-2. Purpose. The making of pawn loans and the acquisition and disposition of tangible personal property by and through pawnshops vitally affects the general economy of this State and the public interest and welfare of its citizens. In recognition of these facts, it is the policy of this State and the purpose of the Pawnbrokers Modernization Act of 1989 to: (1) Ensure a sound system of making loans and acquiring and disposing of tangible personal property by and through pawnshops, and to prevent unlawful property transactions, particularly in stolen property, through licensing and regulating pawnbrokers; (2) Provide for licensing fees and investigation fees of licensees; (3) Ensure financial responsibility to the State and the general public; (4) Ensure compliance with federal and State laws; and (5) Assist local governments in the exercise of their police authority. (1989, c. 638, s. 2.)

§ 91A-3. Definitions. As used in this Article, the following definitions shall apply:

(1) "Pawn" or "Pawn transaction" means a written bailment of personal property as security for a debt, redeemable on certain terms within 180 days, unless renewed, and with an implied power of sale on default.

(2) "Pawnbroker" means any person engaged in the business of lending money on the security of pledged goods and who may also purchase merchandise for resale from dealers and traders.

(3)....

§ 91A-5. License required. It is unlawful for any person, firm, or corporation to establish or conduct a business of pawnbroker unless such person, firm, or corporation has procured a license to conduct business in compliance with the requirements of this Chapter. (1989, c. 638, s. 2.)

Chapter 4

Practice Set 4.1

(1) N.C. Const. art. II, § 11

(2) U.S. Const. amend. I

(3) U.S. Const. art. I, § 2, cl. 5

(4) N.C. Const. art. 14, § 1

(5) N.C. Const. art. 1, § 19

Practice Set 4.2

(1) Chapter 93A, section 6(a)

(2) Chapter 25, section 2-101.

Practice Set 4.3

N.C. Gen. Stat. § 14-11 (2003)

Practice Set 4.4

S.C. Code Ann. § 31-21-10 (Law. Co-op. 2004)

Practice Set 4.5

(1) 15 U.S.C. § 1001 (1994)

(2) 15 U.S.C.A. § 1001 (West 1997)

(3) 15 U.S.C.S. § 1001 (LexisNexis 1997)

Practice Set 4.6

N.C. Gen. Stat. §§ 90-179 to -187.15 (2003).

Practice Set 4.7

N.C. Gen. Stat. §§ 90-182, -185, -187 (2003).

Chapter 6

Practice Set 6.1

Shorten the following case names in accordance with *Bluebook* rules 10.2.1. and 10.2.2:

1. *Claude Hooks, A.G. Goins, D. J. Powell, D. J. Shelly, Elwood Robinson, Mickey Long, Cecil Gurkin, H.H. Collins, Henry Merritt, Luther High, and Daniel M. Spell, Officers and Trustees of Smyrna Baptist Church v. International Speedways, Incorporated and Marie D. Carter*

    Hooks v. Int'l Speedways, Inc.

2. *Texaco, Inc., Petitioner v. Ricky Hasbrouck, dba Rick's Texaco, et al.*

    Texaco, Inc. v. Hasbrouck

3. *State of North Carolina, Plaintiff-Appellee/Cross Appellant v. Daniel J. Krim, Defendant-Appellant/Cross Appellee (assume this case was heard in a North Carolina court.)*

    State v. Krim

4. *In re the Estate of Lois v. Greenheck, Deceased*

    In re the Estate of Lois v. Greenheck (omission of "the" is arguable under Rule 10.2.1(d)).

5. *Chase Bryant and Charles Bryant v. Independent School District No. 1-38 of Great County, North Carolina, a.k.a. Reallygood Public Schools*

    Bryant v. Indep. Sch. Dist. No. 1-38 ("No." is abbreviated per 10.2.1—¶ before (a))

Practice Set 6.2

1. Cite <u>Renwick v. News and Observer</u>, 310 N.C. 312, 312 S.E.2d 405 (1984) in *Bluebook* form but without using parallel cites.

    <u>Renwick v. News and Observer</u>, 312 S.E.2d 405 (N.C. 1984)

2. Cite the case <u>In re Dixon</u> in *Bluebook* form. It was decided in 1993 and appears in volume 112 of the North Carolina Court of Appeals reporter on page 248, and in volume 435 of the *South Eastern Reporter, 2d Series* on page 352.

    A) With parallel cites:

    <u>In re Dixon</u>, 112 N.C. App. 248, 435 S.E.2d 352 (1993)

    B) Without parallel cites:

    <u>In re Dixon</u>, 435 S.E.2d 352 (N.C. Ct. App. 1993)

3. Cite the case of <u>State v. Smith</u> in *Bluebook* form. It was decided in 1953 and appears in volume 73 of the *South Eastern Reporter, 2d Series* on page 901, and in volume 236 of the *Supreme Court Reports* on page 748.

    A) With parallel cites:

State v. Smith, 236 N.C. 748, 73 S.E.2d 901 (1953)

B) Without parallel cites:

State v. Smith, 73 S.E.2d 901 (N.C. 1953)

Practice Set 6.3

1. Cite the case of Home Port Rentals, Inc. v. Ruben, from the fourth circuit in 1992. The case is reported in volume 957 of the *Federal Reporter, 2d Series* starting on page 126.

    Home Port Rentals, Inc. Reben, 957 F.2d 126 (4th Cir. 1992)

2. Cite the fourth circuit decision in United States v. Hylton, appearing on page 781 of the *Federal Reporter, 3d Series*, volume 349.

    United States v. Hylth, 349 F.3d 781 (4th Cir. 2003)

Practice Set 6.4

1. Cite the case appearing on page 293 of the Federal Supplement, volume 759, entitled, "Haburjack v. Prudential Bache Securities, Inc." It was decided in 1991 and came from the Western District of North Carolina.

    Haburjack v. Prudential Bache Sec., Inc,, 759 F. Supp. 293 (W.D.N.C. 2000)

2. Cite the case of Swain Island Club, Inc. v. White, coming out of the Eastern District of North Carolina in 1953, and appearing in volume 114 of the Federal Supplement on page 95.

    Swain Island Club, Inc. v. White, 114 F. Supp. 95 (E.D.N.C. 1953)

Chapter 10

Practice Set 10.1

Look at the sample *Shepard's* page reprinted as Figure 10.1. Can you find the case reported in 310 N.C. 312? Can you find the case reported in 310 N.C. 384?

What is the name of the case beginning on page 384?

>   North Carolina v. Watson

When was it decided?

>   1984

Practice Set 10.2

Using the sample *Shepard's* page provided above, Shepardize the case of *North Carolina v. Hinnant*, 310 N.C. 310, for the following:

1. What is the parallel citation?

    312 S.E.2d 653

2. Is there any subsequent history? If so, list the citation(s):

    No.

3. Is there any prior history? If so, list the citation(s) and then translate what it means:

    s 65NCA130: same case, 65 N.C. App. 130

4. Give a full *Bluebook* citation to the case using parallel citations, and including any subsequent history:

    ***North Carolina v. Hinnant*, 310 N.C. 310, 312 S.E.2d 653 (1984)**

5. What is the first entry in the "treatment" section?

    319NC455

6. How many citing cases are listed from the Supreme Court? **__0__** Court of Appeals? **__6__**

7. What does the last entry in the list mean?

    ***Hinnant* is cited in volume 28 of the Wake Forest Law Review on page 547.**

8. According to just the *Shepard's* page depicted in Figure 1, is the *Hinnant* case good law?

    Yes.

Chapter 12

Practice Set 12.1

The issue could be phrased a variety of ways. Here is one example. Note that it includes facts as well as the legal issue.

Under the law of equitable distribution, is a wife entitled to a portion of her husband's small business based upon her 17 years of work in exchange for a share of its profits during the marriage?

Index